Arabian Fantasy

Arabian Fantasy

Herbert Chappell

Photographs by
Robin Constable

NAMARA PUBLICATIONS | QUARTET BOOKS   LONDON

Reflection of an oil pump

First published in 1976 by
Quartet Books Limited
a Member of the Namara Group
27 Goodge Street, London W1P 1FD

Copyright © 1976 by
Namara Publications Limited

ISBN 0 7043 2129 7

Design by Mike Jarvis

Printed in Great Britain by
Gavin Martin Limited, Wallington, Surrey
and Anchor Press Limited of Tiptree, Essex

Resting pearl diver

Contents

Pearl divers

with affection,
gratitude and respect,
this book is dedicated to
THE PEARL DIVERS
OF BAHRAIN

In Darkest London

'BAHRAIN?' he asked. 'Shall I tell you about Bahrain?'

He leaned towards me, his elbows denting the elegant blotter. Outside in Hyde Park a group of Horse Guards trotted past the window, harness jingling and breastplates glinting in the wintry sun. It was late November. At that moment the Knightsbridge office in the heart of London seemed light-years removed from a tiny island in the Arabian Gulf.

'I tell you, most people who go to Bahrain look at nothing but the inside of the transit lounge. They arrive in the middle of the night, change planes, see nothing and complain about the heat! But if you are lucky and reach Bahrain in the daytime, then you will see the island from the air. Believe me, that is an astonishing sight; the bright gold of the desert sand with a rim of silver and creamy white where the salt-marshes merge with the shallow blue water of the Gulf. Lying there, the island looks exactly like the shell of an oyster.'

Very slowly Naim Attallah unclasped his fingers and laid his hands – palms downwards – on the acre of polished desk.

'Herbert,' he whispered, 'I want you to go and open the oyster. Who knows, inside you may find a pearl.'

I WALKED THROUGH the outer office past the babble of telephones and the chattering of the Telex into the frantic din of the rush hour. With no hope of getting a taxi I wandered through Kensington Gardens trying to size up my meeting with Naim Attallah, listing in my mind the jumble of enthusiasms he had thrown at me. *Arabian Fantasy* within only a few weeks had grown from a mere idea to an ambitious and complex project. There was to be a film which I was to direct, a book which I was to write and – already – a record album due for release the following month.

The music on that record was the starting point for the entire project. Pearl or no pearl I should be working once again with its composer, the monstrous Fanshawe!

I thought back a couple of years to my first, shattering meeting with Fanshawe. Purely by chance I had caught the last few seconds of a radio programme – a burst of wild, exalted music. There was a pause, followed by the announcer's hushed tones: '. . . and that was David Fanshawe, composer and explorer, talking about "*African Sanctus*".'

Intrigued, I dialled his number. He picked up the telephone before it had chance to ring and boomed, 'Fanshawe speaking'.

'I've just this minute heard some of your music on the radio,' I began, somewhat taken aback by the speed of his reply.

'Lost a lot of oomph!' he grunted. 'Typical BBC!'

'Didn't sound too bad this end. I produce television programmes.'

'Thought you were a composer,' he said.

'I am. And I'd like to talk to you about it.'

'Fine,' he boomed again. 'Come round and have a listen. See you in ten minutes. I'll show you a picture of me on a camel.'

As conversations go, it was a little light on charm. Fanshawe, I gathered, was not one to waste time.

All that I had heard of his music amounted to ten seconds at the most. But being a composer myself I was curious at the way he had integrated recordings of 'live' African music within his own original musical setting of the Latin Mass. The duality struck me as instantly attractive, impressive and direct. Those few seconds of music seemed to possess the one vital ingredient essential to a television programme; I wanted to know more.

What would he look like, this 'musical Livingstone'? Driving across Barnes Common I had visions of native bearers on the South Circular Road, Fanshawe borne aloft with solar topee and fly-swat, hacking a path through the traffic jam at East Sheen.

Colonial habits die hard and the idea became increasingly incongruous as I drew up outside a row of regimented and slightly seedy terraced houses, each with its identical bay window and curlicews. Those Edwardian architects had built to last, and the neat little houses possessed an aura of quietly assured respectability; an age when God was happy to smile on the Empire, for wasn't he – as everyone knows – an Englishman?

At one end of the road, letting down the tone, was a used-car showroom guarded by an alsatian and an evil looking man with a thin black moustache, the breast pocket of his white coat stained by innumerable ball-point pens.

At the far end of the terrace was the entrance to a cemetery with a space for the hearses to turn round. Beyond the wall, only a few yards away, the mortal remains of the great explorer Sir Richard Burton rested uneasily in a bizarre tomb fashioned in stone like an Arab tent.

Despite that, Avenue Gardens, East Sheen, London S.W.14, did not look too much like Africa. Burton had charted the course of the Nile; Fanshawe had done the same, only musically with a tape recorder.

It all seemed totally appropriate. Every explorer has to start and end somewhere. Avenue Gardens was as good a place as any.

'It's O.K. Potting!' boomed the voice from behind the front door. 'I'll answer it. Must be the man from the Beeb.'

Fanshawe proved to be largely as I had imagined him. But he was dressed not in a solar topee, but a dog-eared knitted peaked cap, baggy lovat trousers, thick woollen socks and sandals. Tall, overweight, with a youthful and chubby face, the over-all impression was at once pompous, humble and immensely likeable. Billy Bunter was alive and well and living in 6, Avenue Gardens, East Sheen.

'Come in. Come in. Shan't be a minute. I'm just on the phone to *Time Life*. They want to do a telly series about me.'

Then he bawled from the foot of the stairs, 'Potting! Potting! What time is the man coming from *Readers' Digest*?'

True or not, I was amazed at the transparent arrogance of the man, playing off one TV producer against another, name dropping in every direction before I was even inside his door, which bore the legend: 'No advertising literature.'

After a moment or two he finished his phone call and ushered me up the narrow staircase.

'It's all happening,' he thundered. 'Five years' work. All coming to fruition at once. Fantastic. And about bloody time. They won't know what's hit them. My record. My book. My American tour . . .' He babbled on in a torrent of egotism, hustling me up the stairs and pausing only to bellow, 'Tea, Potting. Tea! *Jambo! Jambo!*'

Briskly he clapped his hands twice. In the shadows at the far end of the passage something shuffled and moaned.

Potting, I concluded, must be one of his native

bearers. On the walls were various tribal trinkets; African beads, ornaments, knives. A fierce tribal mask glowered at me and I stepped back hurriedly, treading on one of his sandals. Fanshawe did not even notice and proceeded with his catalogue of triumphs.

'The publishers are going wild about my book. The disc is an absolute knockout. I'll get a test pressing flown over to you from Holland. They say *African Sanctus* will make Bernstein's Mass sound like a Sunday School picnic. Sit down there. I've got the tape all set up ready for you.'

He waved me into a chair already positioned precisely equidistant between two gigantic loudspeakers, hitched up his lovat trousers, yelled 'Tea, Potter. Tea!' and, with a flourish, pressed the replay button on his Stellavox tape machine.

Instantly, the eight thundering fortissimo drum beats that herald *African Sanctus* hammered me into my seat.

The volume in that small room was indescribable. A Masai necklace rattled on the wall. I cringed and Fanshawe looked at me inquisitively. He shouted something. But although I could see his lips move, the onslaught of the music obliterated everything. Nailed to my chair, I was trapped by this maniac at Avenue Gardens, East Sheen, pulsated with tribal frenzy. Our attempts at conversation were pathetic:

'I beg your pardon?' I yelled.

(*San-han-hanctus . . .*)

'What?' he yelled back, over the din.

(*De-he-heus . . .*)

'I said, "What did you say?"'

(More percussion, *fortissimo . . .*)

'Is it loud enough for you?'

(*Do-ho-ho-ho-hominus . . .*)

'Of course it bloody is!'

After a few minutes the first track ended leaving me in a state of shock. There was a quiet tapping on the door.

'Aha,' said Fanshawe, 'That will be Potting with the tea.' He switched off the tape and thundered, 'Come, Potipha! Enter, Potty!'

Potter. Potting. Potipha. Already three names had cropped up. Were there three separate servants, or just one huge one?

'Enter, Potting!' he bellowed, clapping his hands. And in walked a pretty, English blonde.

'This,' he beamed, 'is my wife, Judith. Potty, Potting or Potipha, for short. You see, she used to have a potting shed . . .'

'Oh, Fanshawe, do shut up,' she said and hovered in the doorway with the tea tray. Turning to me, she said in her classic Home Counties tones, 'Fanshawe does tend to go on a bit, y'know!'

Still dazed and with my ears ringing, I felt this casual remark from Judith summed up the entire episode and provided an explanation. With wifely resignation at the maniac she had married, her reaction imposed some degree of sense on the whole thing. Yes. She was right. The man did indeed go on a bit. Fanshawe was without a shadow of doubt egocentric and apparently insensitive to anybody else's feelings. But why?

As we listened to the rest of *African Sanctus* – with the volume turned down to a reasonable level – David Fanshawe, bit by bit, provided his own answer. Beneath the arrogant pomposity all was not quite as rosy as he pretended. Since his days at Music College he had tramped around Africa, always penniless and frequently seriously ill. From Dover Docks he had hitch-hiked or walked thousands of miles; through Europe, Turkey, Saudi Arabia and most of the Middle East. From Cairo he had followed the course of the Nile through the Sudan to Lake Victoria, through Kenya, Tanzania and Uganda. He, with Judith picking up the pieces, had pushed forward with a superhuman mania to record the dying music of Africa, despite opposition from officialdom, imprisonment, dysentery, malaria, and every other hazard. Suspicious police had confiscated his tapes, bugged his room, threatened him and obstructed him. To them he was a nutty Englishman. Armed with a tape-recorder and a camera he was very likely a spy. A hippopotamus had upturned his canoe. He had bluffed his way out of Uganda with his Kensington Public Library ticket. He had learned not to take No for an answer.

After five years collecting tape recordings of African music he had settled down to compose a large-scale setting of the Latin Mass, merging his own musical ideas with the sounds on the tapes. As I listened to the result, I was bowled over, not so much by the technical skill which was sometimes flimsy, but by the musicality, the sincerity and the sheer hard slog of it all. I decided there and then to turn it into a television film.

At the door I reassured David that come what may *African Sanctus* would be a brilliant film.

'D'you think so?' he said touchingly. 'D'you really think so?'

I drove away past the used-car salesman and the snarling alsatian and David yelled after me.

'Once you've made *Sanctus*, can we do a film about Bahrain? It's a fantastic place. Date pickers' songs. Pearl divers. Glugging noises from the oil wells . . . Bahrain has everything, I tell you!'

In the driving mirror I could still see him shouting after me, his arm around Judith.

'I even got my wife there!' he yelled from the door-step. 'Isn't that right, Potting?'

'Oh, Fanshawe. Do belt up,' she said as she waved cheerio.

All the Perfumes
of Suburbia

'LIVER,' said Fanshawe.

'*Lee-vaire*,' he insisted, grotesquely exaggerating every movement of lips and tongue. The pretty Gulf-Air stewardess smiled gently as if to comfort him. Fanshawe eyed the duty-free drinks trolley with longing. Much to his credit he avoided all temptation.

The same could be said for the Gulf-Air stewardess. Due, no doubt, to the efficiency of her basic-training she carried on smiling. In fact she barely winced at all, even when Fanshawe – as if in evidence – prodded her fiercely in the midriff.

'*Lee-vaire*,' he repeated, this time with greater volume, convinced – as are all Englishmen abroad – that anybody encountered south of Dover is both simple-minded and hard of hearing.

Around us, in an ever spreading penumbra of embarrassment, passengers of every nationality buried their heads in *Punch*, *Le Monde*, *The New York Times*, the in-flight menu and the instruction card which tells you where to find your life-jacket, should you ever need to.

The Gulf-Air stewardess attempted to push the drinks trolley to the next row of passengers but Fanshawe grabbed her dramatically by the elbow.

'Anything stronger than a Coke and I'm a gonner,' he confided, and told her about *African Sanctus*.

'It was a great film. I don't deny that. And you directed it brilliantly,' he said, pointing me out as a hard-hearted villain, 'but you really put me through it!'

Trapped, the stewardess stood there patiently. She had no alternative. Fanshawe's paralysing grip on her elbow saw to that.

'In the Sudan he nearly finished me off for good!' On he rambled, recounting the merciless way I had submitted him to the perils of malaria, typhus, beri-beri and Khartoum Zoom in my maniac trot with Fanshawe and a BBC film crew from one end of the Nile to the other, and how we were so jolly lucky he had any liver left and was, indeed, alive at all.

'The dear girl doesn't understand a word I'm talking about,' said Fanshawe, releasing his grip on the stewardess.

'On the contrary, sir,' she replied in perfect English, 'you have my greatest sympathy. For my uncle has dreadful trouble with his liver too – and he only lives in East Wittering.'

'East Wittering? Well, there's a coincidence,' said Fanshawe with renewed enthusiasm. 'Used to go there every single summer when I was a child. We used to stay at a little cottage . . .'

But by then both trolley and stewardess had moved on and I pretended to snooze gently.

In a way he was right to complain about me. *African Sanctus* had been a complex and difficult undertaking. But that was a year ago – and *Sanctus*, which had received rave notices when televised in England and America, was well and truly behind us.

Or was it? Perhaps I had let myself in for a fresh range of horror; once again I was directing a film about Fanshawe and his music. *Arabian Fantasy* was under way and it was too late to turn back now. Already Fanshawe and I were on the Gulf-Air jet, heading for Bahrain, on our pre-production recce.

Arabian Fantasy had been set up in record time. Only a few weeks had elapsed since my initial meeting in the Namara office in Knightsbridge. At that stage *Arabian Fantasy* had been just that – a fantasy – yet one more idea for a film. Now it was a hard fact and in the coming week my Bahrain recce would, hopefully, give me the information I needed to write the script, to create a financially valid shooting schedule, select locations, make arrangements with officials, ministries, local musicians, pearl divers . . . It was a fearsome task and time was against us.

The VC-10 hummed onwards over Istanbul, the

18

Bosphorus, Turkey and Cyprus. These magical names filled me with apprehension. The closer we got to Bahrain, the less I realised I knew about it.

'Last time I went to Bahrain,' said Fanshawe, 'I ruddy well hitch-hiked; overland via Teheran, Sophia, Istanbul, Kuwait and so on. None of this luxurious jet-travel. I was penniless and on my own. And when I got there I only had 100 dinars and I spent it all on rounding up a bunch of pearl divers, getting them to sing me their songs so that I could record them on my crummy old cassette. One hundred dinars – it seemed to me then like a fortune. But after me Disney went there and used them in some film about pirates. He gave them 5,000 dollars. By now I bet the pearl divers – if any of them still exist – will want the key to the Bank of England before they'll so much as open their mouths. If, that is – and it's a big If – if any pearl divers still exist.'

'Don't be so depressed,' I said. 'I'll find every pearl diver who's ever gulped water. Leave it to me. *Arabian Fantasy* – just like *African Sanctus* – will be a knockout of a film. I promise you.'

Fanshawe, only slightly reassured, and still thinking of his liver, nodded off to sleep.

To our right the late afternoon sun began to sink into the endless expanse of fluffy white cloud which stretched beneath us in every direction like the surface of some gigantic soufflé. The Gulf-Air jet throbbed its way across Iraq and the soufflé changed colour far too quick for reality. Like a badly graded film it turned progressively to orange mousse, then lavender, grey and – suddenly – black.

Ahead of us, in the darkness, lay Bahrain.

'Beg pardon?' said Fanshawe drowsily.

'I said "Ahead of us, in the darkness, lay Bahrain". Not bad, eh? Rather a good line for my book.'

'Rubbish!' said Fanshawe. Stretching his arms with a yawn, he pressed the button above his head and ordered another liver-proof Coke.

He was right to deflate me. At that stage I had no justification for waxing lyrical about Bahrain. Unlike Fanshawe, who had visited the island many times, I'd never so much as been there. Despite that, I had inevitably built up in my mind a picture of Bahrain, or tried to. But what little knowledge I had was so full of inconsistencies that I was incapable of creating any coherent picture in my imagination.

I knew there were still a few pearl divers who rummaged on the oyster beds in the same centuries-old way, equipped with nothing more scientific than a nose-clip shaped like a tiny wish-bone. Yet I also knew that Bahrain had the most advanced aluminium works in the world, that the island processed massive quantities of oil, that its wealth – quite small when compared to that of some of the other Arab states – was still sufficient to make the country economically sound. I knew that the island of Bahrain was tiny and that ninety-per-cent of it was desert. Yet, at the same time, it boasted one of the most up-to-date airports in the world.

Airport. The very thought made me shudder. Not that the actual landing ever worries me; it doesn't. In fact I look forward to the roar of the air-brakes and the momentary scare of touching down on the runway. But I still think Dorothy Parker was right when she said 'If you go by boat, you travel. If you go by air, you are sent.' For the real terrors are not flying, but coping with the airports at either end; that no-man's-land of incoherent Tannoys, surly customs officers, suspicious men in semi-military uniform, their hands always dangling idly by their revolvers, too close for comfort, the bland and disbelieving look on immigration officers' faces as they breathe on their rubber stamps. And always the fretting, dismayed mob of pushing adults and exhausted children, confused and helpless.

Airport buildings, too, never allow any hint of humanity. They are a world of total extremes; either

Blind man in Bahrain street

one thing or another. Enormously big or idiotically small. An impersonal bewildering plastic metropolis like Heathrow that stretches for miles. Or, on the other hand, a strip of sun-baked earth with a wind-sock and a goat tethered to a Coca-Cola machine.

I once saw a herd of goats going through Passport Control at Cairo Airport.

Consequently, not knowing what to expect, Bahrain International Airport came as a pleasant surprise. For one thing, it was almost deserted, spotlessly clean and, best of all, seemed to have no piped music. Our baggage was off the plane almost before we were and the Customs man who inspected our luggage, did it up again and smiled a thank-you.

Our taxi ride, along the three-mile causeway that now links the old island of Muhurraq, provoked endless startled gasps from Fanshawe. 'Good Lord. All this is *new*,' he said as we drove over acres of newly-claimed land where the sea had once lapped on his earlier visits. 'Good Lord. But it's *all new!*' as if nobody had thought to ask his permission first.

The hotel's clientele seemed to consist exclusively of salesmen and representatives of one international corporation or another. Bills were not paid; they were signed. Apart from unfamiliar items printed on the laundry list – mysterious things like *thobes* and *wazars* – the Gulf Hotel could be almost anywhere in the world. Everybody staying there was spending, or dealing in, somebody else's money. Consequently, the public rooms resembled moves on a monopoly board.

In one corner of the Lounge a middle-aged Texan, with a white stetson shielding his eyes and red dungarees tucked into high-heeled cowboy boots, chatted easily with four Japanese.

'He's in here every night,' the barman confided. 'Perhaps he must have seen too many Roy Rogers movies when he was a kid.'

True to form, the Texan loped out of the lounge

with the easy swagger of an old cow-poke, saying 'Time to be movin' on.' The diminutive Japanese bowed him out and then settled down around a coffee table, dealing to each other their respective business-cards many times over, as if they were playing a hand of poker.

At other tables the stakes piled up as this particular desalination scheme was swopped for that road-building contract, or this trading agreement for that government credit. Bahrain is one of the centres of the financial world. In the morning your phone-call to the Far East decides the closing prices in Hong Kong; another phone call in the afternoon catches the New York Stock Exchange the moment the market opens.

With every handshake in the Gulf Hotel, with every rat-trap click of a briefcase, somebody, some-where – the other side of the world, in Zurich, Washington, London or Tokyo – made another few million.

Fanshawe and I looked at each other helplessly. We were in the centre of a world we knew nothing about.

'We're in the wrong business,' said Fanshawe, putting on his whipped-spaniel face, 'We'll never get rich by putting dots on manuscript paper.'

And he stared gloomily at the record cover of *Arabian Fantasy*, due for release in a couple of weeks. It was a beautiful cover. Across the double-spread golden sand dunes inter-twined sinuously, like the thighs of a Bill Brandt nude.

'Tomorrow you must take me around Bahrain and show me those fabulous dunes.'

'What dunes?'

'Those dunes.'

'There aren't any sand dunes in Bahrain,' he replied. I was dumbfounded.

'What do you mean, no dunes?' Whistling the first few bars of *Lawrence of Arabia* I spread out my hands like the main title on a cinerama screen.

'No sand dunes in Bahrain,' he said sipping his Coke and adding hopefully, 'but there is a little rim of rock down in the oil-field.'

'My dear Fanshawe. How can you possibly have a film called *Arabian Fantasy* and *not* have sand dunes?'

I grabbed the record sleeve from him and pointed at it dramatically. Unmistakably and large as life was a photo of D. Fanshawe, posing in full desert gear, his head swimming in a halo of sunlight.

'Look!' I said. 'Is that, or is that not, a Bahrain sand dune you are standing on?'

'Well, not really . . .' he said, shifting sheepishly in his chair. 'We took that photo, actually, at Camber Sands on the south coast of England, not far from Folkestone.'

'Now you tell me.'

'And those rolling dunes there . . .' he said, pointing to the double-page spread, 'those were photographed in the Liwa, which is on the mainland far away to the south of Bahrain.'

'Well, O.K. Let's forget about sand dunes. Can you show me some Bedouin tomorrow?'

'There aren't any,' said the whipped-spaniel again. 'The Bahrainis have always been town dwellers. They don't live in tents, but houses and apartments. And,' he added guiltily, '. . . they don't, you might as well know, ride around on camels, but in Chevrolets and Cadillacs.'

'And the pearl divers . . .'?

'These days they work in the oil refinery – those that are still alive – or in the aluminium works, or on building sites, or as taxi-drivers.'

This information, delivered with a pathetic resignation, was the biggest blow of all. Sand dunes, Bedouin tents and all the desert paraphernalia, were not really important. Wallpaper, so many pretty pictures – they did not add up to very much, apart from the useful padding you find in every 'ethnic' documentary.

But the pearl divers of Bahrain were of central and paramount importance to my film as I had planned it. Without the pearl divers there was no film.

'I'm sorry,' said David. 'I thought you realised. When I was here seven years ago, the pearl divers were almost a thing of the past. By now they will have completely disappeared.'

'In which case,' I said, 'tomorrow we'll just have to bloody well find them!'

Arabia Felix

WE SAT down to eat, depressed and tired from our journey, with the growing realisation of the problems ahead. With less than a week in which to recce the film, I would be hard pushed to find what I wanted. And *what* did I want? What did I need to find and organise and plan? What – to put it bluntly – was the film *about*?

To be asking myself such a fundamental question at such a late stage seemed preposterous and amateurish to a degree. In less than a month I should be returning with a film crew – to film *what*?

A whistle-stop taxi ride the following morning – one can recce the entire island in only a few hours – did nothing to ease my worries. We left the hotel at dawn because I wanted to see the quality of the early morning light over the fish-traps in the bay – picket fences, shaped like strange keyholes, in the millpond expanse of the shallows.

The light, as I expected, was a cameraman's dream – grey and pink and blissfully soft – and two stops off the end of the exposure meter, I guessed. But there was no sign of fish-traps, only the vague and massive shapes of oil tankers lying at anchor. Where, Fanshawe assured me, endless fishing boats had been moored on his last visit, an enormous dry-dock was nearing completion. The pearl divers' beach at Hidd was a rubbish heap of old Heineken lager cans and, overhead, jets screamed their approach to Muhurraq Airport.

Some parts of Muhurraq still contained the old buildings and faces and people I had hoped for, gnarled and wise and proud. And the markets – like every *souk* on every travel brochure – presented the tried-and-trusty footage one would expect. Endless lines of colourful vegetables and the scent of strange spices, fruit lusher and brighter than the polythene-wrapped versions we are used to.

But, so what? Everything I saw was camera-fodder, everything that corrupts the normal run of documentary filming. For it is always easy and convenient, when filming in a foreign country, to show picturesque poverty, simply because it happens to be photogenic.

I'll give that thirty-five seconds of screen time and even that's stretching it, I thought. Lingering panning shots across black-veiled mums and snotty-nosed urchins are Out!

The rest of the island – only the top right-hand corner is inhabited – was an expanse of desert; bleak, flat for the most part, and not particularly picturesque. Much of it was an oil-field with rusty pipes snaking from one stop-cock to the next, lying on the surface in every direction, feeding, ultimately into the BAPCO refinery or disappearing into the sea towards Saudi Arabia. The only features breaking up the landscape were isolated oil pumps, like objects from a science museum, their arms see-sawing endlessly above the regular throb of a donkey-engine. Occasionally black pools of oil stained the yellow sand.

Dominating the centre of the island was the rocky mass of Jebel Dukhan; on it the space-age dish of a tracking station.

It was still only mid-morning, but already the January sun was directly overhead and the light harsh and flat.

Even that time of the winter gave few shadows to soften the desolation, the craggy outline of the Rim Rock, or the arrogant architecture of the modern buildings, hotels and office blocks, springing up at the north of the island. Moored in the distance, near the man-made causeway that links the business area of Manama with the old quarter of Muhurraq, was a gaunt and gigantic dredger, working constantly, sucking up from the shallows of the Gulf tons of mud and rock, pumping it through huge pipes the

AERIAL VIEW: A LAKE OF OIL

DRILLING PLATFORM

BAHRAIN FROM THE AIR

SATELLITE GROUND STATION

AERIAL VIEW OF THE COASTLINE, BAHRAIN

The satellite ground station

size of railway tunnels and spewing it out again an acre at a time, bleached and dried hard as concrete by the sun.

The place appeared to be one enormous building site. Every other vehicle seemed to be a bulldozer, an earth-moving truck or a mobile crane. Occasionally one caught a glimpse of a traditional Bahraini house, centuries old, its mellow plasterwork richly decorated, the wooden doorways intricately carved with complex, interwoven patterns. Or an old wind-tower *bagdir* – ingeniously designed to provide air-conditioning through natural convection, long before any modern invention.

'So,' I said to David, 'where do we go from here? We seem a little thin on the visuals . . . As films go, this one has all the makings of a very good radio programme.'

Clutching my letter of introduction, I paid off the taxi-driver and arrived for our appointment at the Ministry of Information.

Sheikh Esa Mohammad Al-Khalifa, the Superintendent General, greeted us warmly. He turned out to be the sort of person whose twinkling eyes and innate charm could transform every problem, changing each difficulty into a possibility. Shy, quietly spoken,

and obviously brilliant – intellectually and professionally – his gentle control of the situation was immediately apparent.

I had expected him – without any justification on my part – to be a bureaucrat, or, at best, a remote and disinterested official, whose high rank and social background would make our meeting nothing but a formality. I was wrong. I was especially wrong in assuming his attitude would be that of a civil servant and that he would be too busy with an in-tray of more pressing matters to allow any real, personal concern with my problems.

The opposite was the case. In the outer office I had glimpsed his appointments book on the secretary's desk. I had also realised that Fanshawe and I, as we were ushered in to his panelled office, had jumped the queue of people waiting to see him – people whose business was possibly far more urgent than ours.

But the moment I hinted at my disappointment at the lack of visual interest in what I had seen of the island, I saw the sadness in his flashing brown eyes. With that immediate empathy I was soon to discover to be a quality to be found in so many Arabs, my problems became his problems. He was disappointed that I was disappointed. He was saddened to feel that my first impression of the Bahrain he loved so much – his home, his tradition, his culture – meant so little to me.

He was neither angry, nor affronted that I had sized up his island in a few hours and had dismissed it, in film terms, as a non-runner. Instead, he listened with great patience while I hinted, more and more forcefully, that, if I was to make a film about Fanshawe's music, I would have to search for locations in other parts of Arabia.

As he listened, he played quietly with his worry-beads, and was plainly upset – that I was upset.

Had I been on his side of the desk, had I been in his position, dealing with a disgruntled film director, then without doubt I would have been furious.

As I continued with my criticism, his quiet un-ruffled acceptance cooled me down. Instead of vague complaints that Allah had not made Bahrain more attractive to the view-finder, I moved on to specific problems to do with musicians, practical matters concerning transport, permissions from the Police and the Ministry of Interior, and so on.

Finally, he stood up and looked at his watch.

'I am sorry to be so rude,' he said, 'but may we continue this discussion later? Come to my home this evening. I must hurry now.'

'Thank you, sir, for giving us so much of your time. But I really feel that, to get the sort of locations this film needs, I shall have to fly off tomorrow to Abu Dhabi and the Liwa and possibly even farther afield.'

'If you must, then you must. But I have a feeling I can help you find all you require here in Bahrain, in *Sh'Allah.*'

We walked with him through the outer office and out of the building – which was now totally deserted, for Fanshawe felt we had long overstayed our welcome. As he got into his sand-coloured Mercedes,

he smiled gently at us, saying with genuine concern, 'The Romans, you know, came here a long time ago and I expect *their* first impression too was a little unfavourable. But they grew to love it, and to call it "Arabia Felix". Doesn't that mean "happy"?'

'Yes, sir. I think it does.'

'Then you must be happy too. Now I must hurry, or I shall be late for the kick-off. Bahrain is playing a team from Vienna, you know!' And off he went.

Another Mercedes glided up beside us and the driver, Fanshawe and I discovered, had been instructed by Sheikh Esa to stay with us throughout the entire recce and to drive us wherever we required.

'I am,' he said, flashing a mouthful of brown and golden teeth, 'your disposals!'

A Drop in the Ocean

THAT evening, Sheikh Esa's home – from the outside – looked exactly like any modern English house in the stockbroker belt of Surrey or Sussex and would not have seemed at all out of place in Hayward's Heath or Purley. But inside the house, every piece of furniture, every cushion and ornament,conveyed gentle opulence.

Off gold plates and with little gold knives and forks we ate sweetmeats, and honeyed sago, drank sherbet and mint tea from dolls-house cups, while Esa lit a dish of incense.

'I have asked Khalifa Shaheen to join us and show us the film he made of Bahrain's First National Day.'

On cue, Khalifa arrived and greeted Fanshawe like a long-lost brother. David had often told me about Khalifa, how – on earlier journeys to Bahrain – he had helped David find musicians, had introduced him to this place and that, and had generally kept Fanshawe out of harm's way.

'Yippee!' said Fanshawe, crushing Khalifa in a bear-hug, 'Thank God you're still here in Bahrain. I thought you were in Europe and that we'd have to get by without you.'

Then, turning to me with a smile beaming from ear to ear, Fanshawe said: 'Now all our problems are over. We can relax. Believe me there's nothing Khalifa cannot fix!'

True enough, within a couple of minutes of meeting him, it was obvious that Khalifa was every director's ideal liaison man. Running his own business as a ciné and stills photographer, he knew all the problems attached to scheduling, hiring equipment, lights, lenses and film-stock. More than that, he had acted in films, worked with Disney, shot his own films and knew the business from A to Z.

With a sigh of relief I knew that whatever artistic problems remained, at least Khalifa would be my 'man in Bahrain' and would see to it that arrangements made by me during the recce wouldn't fizzle out by the time I returned with the camera crew, as can so often happen.

My change of attitude must have been apparent to Sheikh Esa who gave me one of those 'I told you so' looks.

'You asked about local folk musicians,' he said. 'I expect Khalifa knows one or two!'

From that point onwards I showered Khalifa with questions and listed some of the arrangements that would have to be made for *Arabian Fantasy*. The first thing to know about the film was that it had to fulfil several distinct functions. In one area it was a visualisation in film terms of a musical score – a score that was already composed and recorded. In that score, Fanshawe – as in *African Sanctus* – had combined his 'own' music with 'field recordings' of traditional musicians.

In addition to tapes of folk music, Fanshawe had used sounds of day-to-day desert life, the noises of an oil refinery and many other ingredients – a musical *collage*, in fact.

But, more especially, *Arabian Fantasy* was to show something of the process of creating music – not in the conventional sense of putting dots on paper, but in treating all sound as potentially musical. So, on this level, the film must show David collecting his taped material, working on it, using multi-track sound treatments, and creating a new piece – a composition in the making, called *Symphony of Pearls and Oil*.

There was yet another dimension. Bahrain, over the years, had played a significant part in Fanshawe's life – musical and personal – and that aspect must knit the film together. In previous visits, when a student at the Royal College of Music, he had come to Bahrain many times. But, on those occasions, his sound-recording equipment consisted of nothing more elaborate than a cheap cassette-recorder. He

School bus

Man smoking his water pipe in the souk

had not been particularly successful, but the sounds he had recorded had found their way into an early work, *Salaams*. It was important that the film should re-trace the problems he had faced on those earlier visits.

But the climax of *Arabian Fantasy*, the most important point of the entire film, must be finding those pearl divers who were still alive, taking them to sea in a pearling dhow, and capturing on film – almost certainly for the last time – the songs of that traditional and rapidly vanishing world.

'That won't be easy,' said Khalifa. 'There are only a few divers left. And they are very old men now – eighty, maybe ninety years old. Most of them haven't been to sea for twenty or thirty years.'

'But they *are* still around, somewhere?' I insisted.

'Perhaps. But even if you find them you will never get them to dive for the cameras. It's winter, you must remember, and the sea is too cold.'

'Then we'll have to warm it up! Otherwise it's likely to be the swimming pool of the Bahrain Hilton!'

Khalifa tugged at his neat beard, looking worried.

Sheikh Esa said, 'Well, that's settled then. In a moment I'll take you to eat at the Awali Club. But, first . . .'

And a wall-full of gold lamé curtains parted to reveal an enormous projection screen.

The films – a conventional record of Bahrain's *1st National Day* – and a travelogue called *Gateway to the Gulf* didn't tell me very much. Khalifa had shot several guards of honour, a great deal of marching and one or two interesting shots of a hobby-horse dance. The junketings ended with a spectacular firework display.

But although the film was clearly made on a limited budget and with restricted technical facilities, there was one astonishing helicopter shot – a rapid descent with a 10mm lens coming in from the sea towards Ras al Barr, the southernmost tip of the island which stretches out from the desert like the tail of a snake.

The steep approach of the helicopter created a fore-shortened effect, collapsing the green and silver salt-flats into the gold of the sand. Naim Attallah had been right. From the air, Bahrain did indeed look like the shell of an oyster. I was still looking for the pearl!

'Is there any possibility,' I asked, 'that I could go up in a helicopter and see the island from the air?'

'Tomorrow all necessary arrangements will be made,' replied Sheikh Esa. It was clear that nothing was impossible. He drove us to the Awali Club, built by BAPCO for its refinery staff; an enormous complex, containing every conceivable facility. It included several restaurants, bars and billiard rooms, a cinema, table tennis, badminton and ten-pin bowling, as if a Mid-West township had been lifted bodily from America to the desert.

As we ate, Sheikh Esa – his traditional Arab dress contrasting oddly with the holiday-camp atmosphere – said, 'Nothing is too good for the workers!' and smiled down at his prawn cocktail.

'Did you know,' he went on, 'that ancient Bahrain – Dilmun, it was called then – was known as the Garden of Eden? Noah came here, they say, after The Flood. Abraham himself was born not far away. Wasn't that sensible of him!'

He talked about the ancient world of Bahrain, the archaeologist's paradise, and the modern world of communications, finance, oil and industry. As he talked, his innate love for the island drove the evening forward, his enthusiasm for the landscape and the people, for the old ways of life and the new, providing a compulsive picture of the ancient and the modern.

Pearl divers

Boys playing football

Bus stop

'Before you return to London, I must tell you about Gilgamesh and the "Flowers of Immortality", and many other things. I tell you what; on Thursday afternoon I shall instruct my Secretary to cancel all my arrangements and I shall take you myself into the desert. I promise, you will then understand Bahrain, for you will see those things that businessmen and visitors never have time to see.'

In the car-park a sudden gust of wind sprang up.

'It is the *shamaal*,' he said, wrapping his white cotton *guttra* across his face to keep out the dust. 'You can expect it this time of year. And you *really* want to go pearl diving in this wind?'

Another group, an Arab family also leaving the club, heads bowed over against the wind, barged straight into us. The mother's umbrella snapped inside out and her daughters – their long black *abas* flapping wildly – spun around like bats out of control.

'Rather you than me!' shouted Esa as he drove off.

Perhaps he's got something there, I thought. I watched the Arab family flutter their way to their car and was intrigued to see that under their traditional black shawls the mother and her daughters wore a highly-coloured selection of western woollies, the sort you can buy in any shop in Oxford Street.

'If it's like this tomorrow, it'll be too gusty for a helicopter,' said Khalifa, driving us back to our hotel in his Falcon Cinefoto minibus. 'And in any case there's plenty of things about the island you should know.'

He was a fund of information. More important than providing me with mere facts, his intricate knowledge of Bahrain and Bahrainis stopped me putting my foot in it on many occasions.

'You must realise,' he said, 'Bahrain may only be a dot on the map, the size of the Isle of Wight, but its importance, commercially and as a centre of communications, is absolutely enormous. And,' he added, 'we may be an independent Arab State, but we are not at all rich, compared to Saudi, Kuwait and others. All the same,' he added, winking broadly, 'we're not doing too bad!'

To our right the twin minarets of the Issa Town Mosque twinkled in the distance, outlined in fairy-lights. Also to our right, a cluster of fireflies in the darkness, lay the massive processing plant of the BAPCO oil refinery, the mast-head lights twinkling on the tankers moored off Sitra Jetty and the single flare of the ALBA aluminium plant – one solitary untamed jet of excess gas, its iridescent blue flame roaring at the black sky like the bunsen burner in some giant chemistry set. These were only the external signs of an island – however small – doing very nicely thank you.

Driving us back to our hotel, Khalifa asked us as much about England as we asked him about Bahrain. He had worked in England, had married a Brighton girl and was a confirmed anglophile. Had he not, indeed, worked with none other than Shirley Bassey?

He told me how it was only since August 1971 that Bahrain had become an independent state and subsequently a member of the United Nations and of the Arab League. Before then, through a long series of complex military and political agreements, Britain had been responsible for matters of foreign policy and defence for a century and a half.

I couldn't help wondering what the prancing clowns of Westminster had made of it all when they acquired Bahrain from the remains of the old East India Co. in 1820. Very likely those parliamentary faces had registered exactly the same blank look of incomprehension as when we gave it all back again, East of Suez, in the 1970s.

'These days,' said Khalifa, 'we are basically on our own – with a little help from our friends! It has its

'Not any more. Japanese cultured pearls killed off the market in the 30s – and the Depression didn't help. But at the very same time, in 1932, we discovered oil in Bahrain,' and he patted the dashboard of the minibus affectionately. 'Little black pearl of the desert, you came just in time.'

'Does Bahrain produce much oil?'

'A drop in the ocean, compared to our neighbours! So, if we don't produce so much of our own, we process one hell of a lot of theirs!'

'And what happens when theirs runs out?'

'Well, by then it won't matter. By the time Arab oil is exhausted, Bahrain will have dozens of other things – the aluminium, communications, international banking and so on. And by then we shall have bought up the rest of the world anyway! And . . .' he added mischievously, '. . . we'll save you a teeny little bit of the Tower of London, if you're very good, as a souvenir!'

We drew up in front of the Gulf Hotel and thanked him for the lift.

'He's bloody right, you know,' said Fanshawe. And the automatic glass doors of the Gulf Hotel purred apart, something I found distinctly unnerving. I wondered how many people will get their feet wet next time, crossing the Red Sea.

advantages. We don't believe in Income Tax or Profits Tax, so we aren't all strangled at birth like you are in England. And so we can welcome all sorts of ideas and let them flourish here. And if you're thinking of starting up a business here, fine; it doesn't matter who you are. Provided you're certain you can make a go of it, you'll get all the cooperation you need.'

As interesting as all this undoubtedly was, our hotel was getting nearer and nearer and I tried to switch the conversation back to the pearl divers.

'Does any wealth still come into Bahrain from the pearling industry?' I asked. But Khalifa had the bit between his teeth and couldn't be distracted.

Pipe Dream

IN THE few days that remained of our recce, whatever preconceptions I had formed of Bahrain were completely shattered. I had expected the island to represent both the traditional, disappearing Arab world and also the modern, side by side. But I had been totally unprepared for such extreme contrasts. It wasn't so much the so-called 'camel to 'Cadillac' notion that confused me, but the differences between the old people and the young, the black veiled 'purdah' idea where women in outlying date villages would scuttle away from a camera and the swinging, trouser-suited secretaries, immaculately groomed and highly educated, liberated and sophisticated as any Oxford Street *Temp*.

Bahrain, as Khalifa had told me, is perhaps not as innately wealthy as the other Sheikhdoms, but its attitudes are infinitely more attuned to the future. Bahrain was the first of the Arab States to find oil. With that flying start, Bahrain has been a front-runner ever since. The present Amir, H. H. Sheikh Issa bin Sulman al-Khalifa, has greatly extended the programmes of development started by his father. Today Bahrain is a leader in the Arab world in many social, educational and medical areas.

It also made other claims that Bahrainis are justly proud of, that education and health facilities account for over fifty-per-cent of government expenditure in an average year, that free education for both boys and girls had been available since the 1920s, and that advanced technical training for teachers, doctors and scientists is readily available to anyone who wishes to follow specific skills in Bahrain, or through scholarships to other countries' colleges, universities and business schools.

'The trouble is,' said Khalifa, when we met him at his Falcon Cinefoto studio the following morning, 'the trouble is that everybody in Bahrain has so many degrees and letters after his name, you can never find anybody who's prepared to change a washer on your tap for you. I don't know what is worse, a country of illiterate camel boys or a country of Ph.D.s. So, like in England, it's only immigrants who are prepared to get their hands dirty and carry out the unpleasant day-to-day jobs to keep the place ticking over. If it weren't for foreigners the whole island would seize up in no time.'

He laced up a film in the projection room and ran it down to the end of the 'leader'.

'As for me,' he yelled at us from behind the double-glass window of the projection room, 'I have to do my own dirty work. Has anybody seen my hammer?'

He grabbed a hand-towel from the wash-basin and with one single and satisfying blow smashed the glass window of the projection booth.

'I've been wanting to do that for a long time,' he smiled. 'You see you get a *much* better picture with that glass out of the way! The bit I want to show you comes up in just a minute.'

The black and white newsreel, which Khalifa had made with the BAPCO film unit in 1968, flickered before us. An Arabic commentary chuntered on through predictable shots of sheikhs laying foundation stones, distinguished visitors inspecting guards of honour, and so on. I was beginning to doze off when the arabic commentator slipped in the name 'Derveed Fine-showery'. On the projection screen before us, cavorting with a mob of Bahraini schoolchildren was a younger and certainly thinner Fanshawe. Like the Pied Piper of Bahrain, Fanshawe danced around dangling the microphone of a little cassette recorder as if it were a used tea bag. All around him dozens of little Arab children armed with every conceivable traditional instrument, blew, scraped and banged – or pretended to.

'D'you know,' said David, '(God, I was thinner

Camel driver

then!) D'you know that I found all those old traditional instruments inside a school and not one of those children had the slightest idea how to play a single note.'

There were various single- and double-headed drums, a *tamboura* with a pottery body similar to an Egyptian hand-drum, a *kanoun* closely resembling a zither, a couple of *nai* – primitive flutes – and the sort of instrument that is supposed to delight all snakes in a basket, a *zumara*. Despite its dubbed Arabic commentary, the film was shot mute. Even so, one look at the *zumara* and it was easy to understand why it had terrified horses and knights alike when they first encountered it on the Crusades.

'Well, that at least proves the actual traditional instruments are around somewhere,' I said, 'but is there anyone who can still play them . . .?'

'Hang on a moment,' yelled Khalifa through the hole in the wall where the beam of the projector made rainbow patterns refracting off the jagged edges of the broken glass. 'Any minute now and you'll see a traditional Bahraini dance.'

'Whooppee,' I said.

The film flickered and fluttered, which hardly helped. Even so, not in your wildest flights of imagination could you ever describe what came next as a Dance.

A shambling line of half a dozen old men, frayed and shapeless tweed jackets worn over their kaftans, swayed drunkenly to the right. (Pause. Two. Three.) After thinking about it for a moment they did the same movement back to their left. (Pause. Two. Three.) And after another lengthy pause they repeated the same shambling movement.

The end man had a cigarette-end stapled to his lower lip. The youngest of the dancers was at least seventy. The line as a whole looked strangely like a photograph of a dole queue during the Depression.

Camel driver

'It's a very *slow* dance.' I said.

'Well, it gets bloody hot here,' said Fanshawe.

'It's also a very *boring* sort of dance, wouldn't you say?'

'Sometimes the humidity in Bahrain is ninety-percent or more,' Fanshawe added plaintively.

'Apart from its amazing anticipation of Monty Python, wouldn't you say that was the slowest, most boring group of geriatrics having a knees-up that it's possible to imagine?'

'Yes.'

'And is all the traditional Bahraini dancing like that?' I asked as nicely as possible.

Camel driver

'It's never *terribly* lively,' said Khalifa. 'But don't worry, I'll arrange lots of dancers for you. We'll fix it for a Friday when everybody is home on their rest-day from work.'

'But you understand, Khalifa,' I said, 'when I say dancers I mean lots of them. I don't want a handful of old grand-dads with one foot in the grave! I know for a fact that there's a lot of negro music on the island, tucked out of sight maybe, but it's there. Also there are songs about date-picking, Omani camel-boy songs, all sort of things and . . .'

'. . . And you want ten battalions of pearl divers. I know,' said Khalifa, raising the plams of his hands to the ceiling. 'Ready when you are, Mr de Mille!'

We left the Falcon studio and headed for the BAPCO oil refinery which I wanted to see at close quarters. Like Fanshawe, I was intrigued by the huge cylinders, pipes and oil-tanks, and the noise they make when you hit them. Their enormous bulk became increasingly impressive the closer we got. Many of the pipes, like sets of orchestral tubular bells, were painted silver. Others were brilliant yellow, pale blue, or pillar box red. Against the blue clarity of the sky, these colours gave the mundane world of an oil refinery a weird, paint-box, story book charm, like some school primer entitled 'Colour Your Own Oil Refinery' – a charm that probably wears thin very quickly if you have actually to work in the place, as opposed to driving around in the air-conditioned comfort of a white Mercedes.

To my un-scientific eyes, the BAPCO refinery looked as if it could handle enough oil to drive every car in the world. My mind reeled at the statistics; 250,000 barrels per day seemed quite a lot. Then Saudi Arabia, on the other hand, produces 8 *million* per day. Or, to put it another way, the oil royalties earned by Bahrain over the last twenty *years* equals Kuwait's royalties for four *months*.

Over the period since oil was first discovered in Bahrain in the early 30s, one half of the oil royalties have annually been ploughed back into the island in the form of educational, medical and social schemes, public works and new capital equipment. The policy has paid off in terms of the people, the number of schools, clinics and hospitals and the high standards of education and public health – higher than any other state in the Gulf.

The irony is that, rather like the record company who turned down the Beatles, it was actually the dear old British who turned down the opportunity offered to them on a plate by a Major Holmes. He was a New Zealander working for a British prospecting company. Realising there was oil beneath the Bahrain desert he obtained a concession from the Amir as long ago as 1925.

Holmes tried several times, but failed to interest any of the British oil companies. 'Nonsense,' they said, 'there can never be enough oil around to warrant commercial exploitation!' So, after two years of rejection by British companies the Major offered it to the Americans who presumably said 'Gee whizz,' and viewed the situation more favourably.

It took, in all, five years to untangle the complexities of company law – Bahrain at that time being a Protectorate of the British – and to set up BAPCO via Standard Oil. '. . . Had it not been for the enterprise of an American oil company,' the guide-book says, 'which took up the concession after it had been refused by the British, the oil of Bahrain might never have been exploited.'

And now the situation is reversed, and prayers are offered up in the fervent hope that the success of North Sea oil-rigs off Ireland and Scotland will soon create Sheikhdoms amongst the O'Murphys and the McTavishes.

Gilgamesh

FANSHAWE SUDDENLY yelled: 'That's the place!' and grabbed our driver in a Thuggee death lock. With a squeal of brakes we slammed to a halt. But Fanshawe was already out of the car, attacking a row of huge metal pipes with a crow bar.

'Stop it, you maniac!' I cried, running after him. 'Those pipes are under God knows how many pounds pressure per square inch. You'll blow up half of OPEC if you carry on like that!'

Oblivious of the danger, he continued his hammering on the pipes. 'The rhythm of the pearl divers,' he said. The security man, never having been faced before with a similar situation, and with no emergency routine designed for mad Englishmen, ran off to see if help was near.

'D'you recognise it?' yelled David, hitting away in a regular dotted rhythmic pattern. 'That's the rhythm of the pearl divers on oil pipes. The Old Wealth and the New!'

'Sentimental twit! Get back in the car before we all get thrown out.'

But he never did. Instead, while the bemused driver kept at our side in bottom gear, Fanshawe and I experimented by tapping every pipe, drum and metal object in sight, large and small, fat and thin, testing their response as potential percussion instruments.

'Before we come back with the film crew,' I said, 'I want you to go to Len Hunt's Percussion Hire place in London and bring with you to Bahrain every single type of percussion beater that exists – little wooden-knobbed xylophone sticks, big sponge-headed timpani sticks, a *tam-tam* beater, like J. Arthur Rank, snare drum sticks, wooden spoons, the lot!'

'Right,' said Fanshawe, adding a resounding 'SIR ! ! !'

'And then I'll do a sequence where we build up a montage of sound, just from the refinery pipes. It will end with you right up there on the largest oil tank of all, thumping it like a gigantic drum. We'll shoot it as tight as possible from a helicopter, level with your head. If you're not decapitated, we'll start on a tight-shot of your face and zoom out as we crane up, leaving you in the distance like a fly on a biscuit-tin.'

The ALBA aluminium plant was equally spectacular from a filmic point of view. The abstract and totally symmetrical ingots blazed at us in the glaring mid-day sun; a silver, open-air version of Fort Knox. And, stacked for mile after mile, the ingots led the eye to the shimmering horizon and what looked like a mirage hovering in the heat – a space-station tracking dish.

The ALBA plant, we were told by the P.R. man produces the staggering amount of 120,000 metric tons per year.

Again, as when faced by the statistics of the BAPCO oil refinery, all I could reply was 'Well, who would have thought it?'

It also offered some classic 'satanic mills' shots in what was called the Pot Room. There, huge vats of molten metal were poured as easily as a milk jug at a vicarage tea party. The noise was deafening, a twenty-four hour molten hell.

'People get killed off here, sometimes,' said our guide, 'if they don't take care.'

I made a mental memo to the film crew.

'By the way,' he added, 'don't touch anything. It's liable to be hot. Very.'

Our guide came from Australia where the basic alumina originates and he knew about these things.

'There are three shots I want here,' I screamed at him above the roar of a cauldron, 'the door lifting like a curtain on the smelting furnace, your excess-gas flare against the night sky, and a whip-pan across a stack of aluminium ingots.'

'No problem, sport!' he replied and we went back to BAPCO for tomato soup, steak and kidney pie and apple crumble.

Once again I was struck by the oddities of the old world and the new, rubbing shoulders with each other. Before lunch I was at the ALBA works, one of the largest and newest aluminium works in the world, and straight afterwards I was standing ankle deep in wood shavings watching the boat-builders of Manama at work, using simple hand-tools with a pre-Biblical simplicity.

The dhows are built now in exactly the same way as they have been for thousands of years. The only concession to the twentieth century is the use of iron nails instead of wooden dowels. Otherwise everything is just as it's always been. Under a ramshackle, makeshift awning of palm fronds, the carpenters carve and saw and hack and chisel, fashioning the timber more like sculptors than chippies. There are no power-tools. The drills work on the spinning-top principle and are driven with a sort of violin bow. The timbers of the hulks, the teak rib cage of some huge dinosaur, are shaped with scrabble words like ax and adze. Never is it necessary to refer to any blueprint or designer's manual. Every inch of the dhow is hand-built with an instinctive understanding for the personality of that particular strut of timber, that plank and that prow. The finished dhow is a rich golden colour, the wood glistening in its natural tints. Coated with linseed oil it smells like the cricket bat you had at school.

The boats are the same elegant shape which has proved itself over countless centuries, only these days the massive hulls are driven more often by throbbing diesel engines. Apart from that one difference, nothing has really changed. They are made that way for the one good reason: good functional

Dhow building

design, where purpose and construction are one and the same thing.

When the *shamaal* whips up the waves as you head north up the Gulf to Kuwait, or south past Oman and Aden to Mombasa, three thousand miles away, I should imagine you'd be as safe on a Manama dhow as a baby in its cradle. And still, however many giant oil-tankers lurk off Sitra Jetty, much of the traditional day to day cargo of the island comes and goes in these simple wooden vessels.

There's one theory that the Phoenicians originally came from Bahrain before they finally settled much

Dhow building

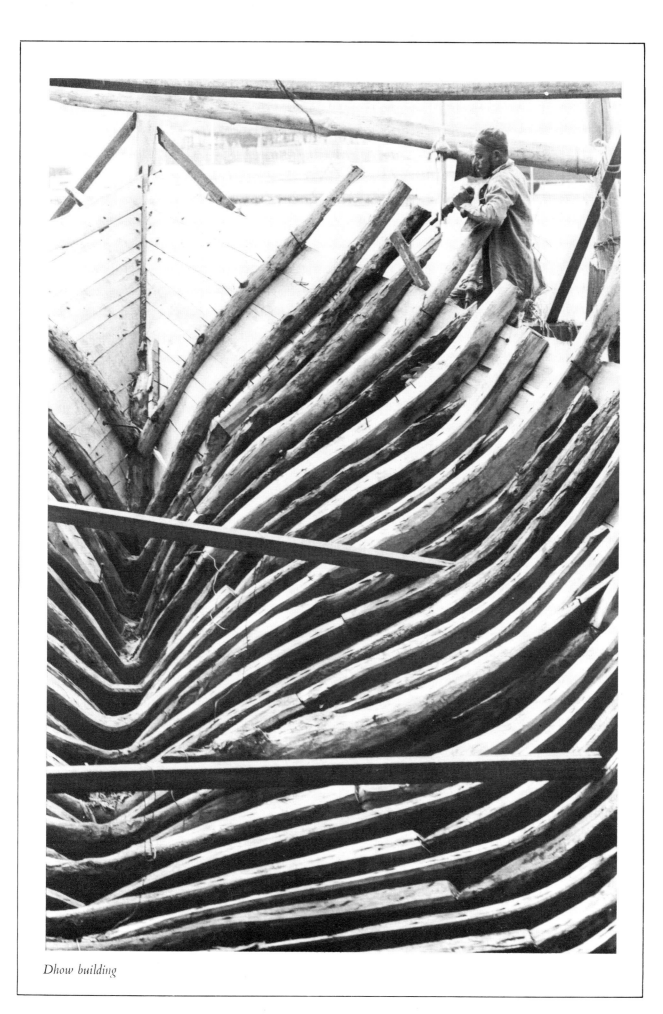

Dhow building

farther up the Gulf on the Euphrates. Whether this is true or not, the wealth and prosperity of Bahrain always came from the sea. Since the dawn of prehistory Bahrainis have always been a nation of seafarers. The wealth of the island, for centuries, lay in trading, fishing and pearling, in the skill of the dhow captains and their knowledge of the winds, the currents and the dangerous, shifting sandbanks. Even today, when a Saudi, Iraqui or Iranian potentate orders a multi-million pound yacht from Europe, complete with every echo-sounder, radar and modern navigational aid, it is an old dhow captain who will be entrusted with its safe passage those last, treacherous few hundred miles from the Tropic of Cancer around Muscat and up through the Gulf to Kuwait.

Because of its geographical position Bahrain has always straddled the trading routes to the Indian Ocean. Five thousand years ago Dilmun, as Bahrain was then known, already figured prominently in the fabled and magical ancient worlds of Babylon, Assyria and Mesopotamia. Precise and business-like records exist, as accurate as any customs declaration, telling of cargoes of rare woods, ivory, gold, the prized green stone Diorite and copper from Oman.

All the wealth of the civilized world it seems flowed through Bahrain. There, traders could find fresh water springs and 'fishes eyes' – as the pearls were called. Inevitably, because of its wealth and strategic importance, the island was bitterly fought over by the power-blocks of Assyria and Persia. It is said that when Sennacherib razed Babylon to the ground in 689 B.C. the debris floated down the Euphrates all the way to Dilmun a thousand miles south. Suitably impressed, the King of Dilmun took the hint and sent back a message by return of post confirming his loyalty!

It was to Dilmun, Sheikh Esa told me, that Gilga-mesh, the semi-mythical king, came in search of immortality. An ancient Babylonian epic recounts how Gilgamesh was instructed to tie a stone to his foot and search on the sea bed for the 'flower of immortality'. If he swallowed it, eternal youth would be his.

Like the pearl divers of Bahrain, who still fix stones to their feet in the same way, he found the 'flower', the elixir of eternal life, believing implicitly in its power, like Cleopatra who drank pearls dissolved in wine.

But, instead of swallowing the flower, Gilgamesh took it home to share with the elders. As he slept, a snake appeared as in Genesis, and ate the pearl, thus cheating Gilgamesh of his immortality. And that is why no snake every grows old, for it sheds its skin and is young again.

The great age of this legend suggests that the pearl diving of Bahrain was known to the civilizations of ancient Babylon and conceivably to others who pre-dated the peoples of the Euphrates. Possibly even to the mysterious culture responsible for the most mysterious feature of Bahrain, the 100,000 tombs that extend across the landscape in the north-west corner of the island, like giant mole-hills, forming the largest prehistoric cemetery in the world.

Beneath each of these gravel mounds – and there are truly tens of thousands of them – lies one or more stone burial chambers. These were constructed not for mass burial, as in Ur or Egypt, but were made to contain one single person. The question is, were these common people, noblemen, or what? Nowhere else in the entire world are similar graves to be found and it is difficult to comprehend a society prepared to give an imposing burial, with all the cost and trouble involved, to ordinary people.

The tombs were robbed many centuries ago, and despite the investigations of a number of archaeo-

David Fanshawe climbs the ancient burial mounds

logists, we have little information to go on other than a few items of pottery, one or two trinkets and, very rarely, an undisturbed skeleton. There are many questions still to be answered, for the whole area is riddled with mystery.

It's an eerie place; especially if you happen to be there at sunset or in the early light of dawn when the sun casts a halo of backlighting and creeps across these 100,000 giant molehills giving them an un-earthly slow-motion animation. It is uncanny how the tombs assume a sort of movement of their own through the way the shadows walk when the sun is low in the sky. So much would depend on the quality of the light and the time of day when eventually we came to shoot there.

Fanshawe had often told me how some of the music of *Salaams* had grown in his imagination out of the sights and sounds of the island. It is always temptingly easy for composers – and critics, especially, who love that sort of thing – to be wise after the event. There is always a seemingly rational facility for hindsight to take over by supplying tangible reasons for every note of the music. Justifications and literal parallels for every melodic turn of phrase are readily available; so are numerous ir-

refutable reasons why such and such a piece of music came to be composed in such and such a way.

But from the moment I first laid eyes on the actual written score of *Salaams*, the physical appearance of the musical notes on the manuscript paper quite clearly related to the topography of the desert landscape. At one point in the score, the musical sound weaved and merged as the womens' voices clustered mysteriously around the unison A-flat for several pages of the score. The look of the page identified with the sound of the music itself; the shape of the music was the shape of the landscape of Bahrain. And just as the music in Fanshawe's imagination at that point had grown out of the lonely and distant calls heard in a date-garden (*Oomi, Oomi* – 'mother') so the graphic shape of the sequence had grown out of the land.

It was important to get this across in the film. Also I had to convey in terms of celluloid, and in as few words as possible, what it felt like to stand there, surrounded by 100,000 man-made hills. I had to reproduce the astonishingly emotive sense of being totally dwarfed by a landscape and at the same time of feeling actually part of it, however insignificant the size of your human scale compared with the epic sense of mortality surrounding you in every direction.

But the 100,000 tombs is the sort of place that means precious little on the screen unless you have some human point of reference, some known and recognisable yardstick of frailty. Only then do you comprehend the relative vastness of the 100,000 tombs as seen through a view-finder and transmitted in the aspect-ratio of a TV screen. You need to relate the expanse and breadth of the site to one tiny, fragile, ephemeral human figure, a Tom-Thumb homunculus, a wind-up Action Man, a plaything of the gods and innocently vulnerable. . . .

'Fanshawe,' I said. 'I want you to lose twenty-five pounds in weight in the next two weeks. Then, provided you're thin enough, I'll pan your sylph-like form as you walk across those tombs into the sunset. Just like John Wayne. And at the same time on the sound track I'll have you rambling on about Life and Art with a capital A.'

'Oh, I say. What fun!' Fanshawe's face positively glowed at the prospect. 'I must say I've always fancied myself doing that sort of thing. Just like they do on the telly.'

Food for Thought

EAGERLY IN his mind Fanshawe made mental notes to go into training to trim his waist line, to stop eating puddings, to get a sun-ray lamp, and to look rugged and handsome like Stewart Granger in *The Snows of Kilimanjaro* and Peter O'Toole after he'd blown up that train in *Lawrence of Arabia*.

'You're right!' he said, bestriding the summit of one of the tombs like the Colossus of Rhodes, hands on hips and dead butch with it. 'I've just *got* to get rid of some of this weight for the telly.'

Then, turning to Khalifa, whose slim and handsome frame, flashing black eyes and neatly trimmed beard put him in the Rudolph Valentino league, Fanshawe said, 'Cor, I wish I was as thin as you!'

He said it with genuine concern. Then he spoiled the effect by adding, 'Cor, I'm terribly hungry. Couldn't we go back to the hotel for a snack?' which we did.

Like so many hotels intent on pleasing all the people all the time, the Gulf's lunch-time menu had pursued international goodwill to the point of aggression. It contained enough intercontinental bonhomie to provoke a diplomatic incident. The 'special' each day bent over backwards in its gesture of friendship, and the chef was clearly so intent on extending hands across the sea as to wrench some arms clean out of their sockets.

Items like *The Great American Cheese Burger* and *Yankee Reveille* jostled against *homos* and *chop suey*. Day by day the taste buds coped with new time-zones, date-lines and jet-lags.

Dimanche à Paris, it said, *coq au vin*. *Montag*, with much slapping of thighs and quaffing of lager, was *wurst Frankfurt*. On Tuesday we were in Naples with *Tagliatelli 'Sophia Loren'*. Wednesdays were Mexican with *Chili con carne* and *Thursday in Down Town Hong Kong* brought *Sweet 'n' sour chicken*. *Friday on Miami Beach* was *sugar-baked Virginia ham, Florida*

peaches, Buttered sweet corn and American Fries, and, to round off the week with true British football and gastromic hooliganism we were offered *Saturday at the Liverpool Kop, Lancashire Hot Pot with pickled red cabbage*.

We settled instead for fish and chips, which, in Bahrain is delicious, since we couldn't remember what day of the week it was. While we ate we scanned the leather-covered, morocco-bound, deeply quilted, astralux-coated, laminated for extra toughness, finger lickin' menu for other goodies and remembered the bad old days in Khartoum when filming *African Sanctus*. The menu there, in the Sudan hotel, made even better reading, containing as it did some quaintly mis-spelt items, including *Foul Roast*, *Foul Cold*, and – for honesty is always the best policy – *Foul Any Style*.

After our grilled *hamor* and chips, I settled for a cup of coffee. Khalifa asked in immaculate cockney for a cup of Rosie Lee. Fanshawe, just to be on the safe side in case he felt peckish later on, rubbed his hands together and leered, 'I don't half fancy a go at that Black Forest Tart over there,' and the lady at the next table puckered her lips and looked at him over her spectacles.

Since there was a definite danger of our late lunch merging into an early tea, I yanked Fanshawe out of the restaurant and we headed for the date-gardens.

'If we're going to include any of *Salaams* in the film I must find some moody visuals *somewhere* on the island,' I said. 'Judging by what I've seen from the road, my best bet is those palm plantations and the little villages around the north-west of the island.'

While everybody in Bahrain possessing an atom of sense snoozed their way through the heat of the afternoon, Khalifa, Fanshawe and I searched through every single date garden from Zallaq to Budaia

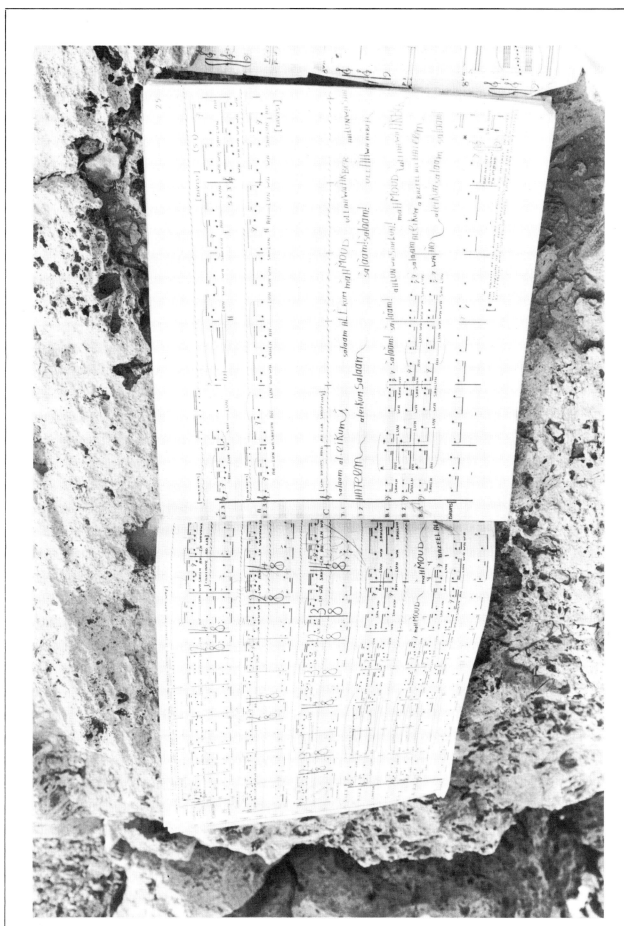

The score of David Fanshawe's Salaams

David Fanshawe reads his score on location

certainly romantic, lush, beautiful and attractive musically. Like so much of Fanshawe's music, it relaxed into a totally endearing delight in the sheer magic of sound textures, the mysterious and utterly overwhelming effect of one well-placed triad, a *doh-me-soh*, in the right context at the right moment. The oldest and most characteristically 'English' trick of all; the juxtaposition of one tonality cutting like a knife against another. Taverner did it in the sixteenth century. So did the Elizabethans, Tallis, Morley, Weelkes and Gibbons. So did Purcell. And, after English composers had eventually stopped aping Europeans and the ghosts of Brahms and Wagner, those same clashes of individually, innocent tonalities conspiring against each other gave a new impetus to English music in the fluency of Benjamin Britten and the gut-wringing honesty of Michael Tippett.

Fanshawe is of this lineage, if, like the rest of us, not in the same league. But his strength as a composer comes from the main-stream confidence in tonality as an expressive force, in its ability, by the flick of a harmony, to make the heart beat faster, the brain to twitch and the hairs to stand up on the back of your neck. That, as far as I am concerned, is what composing is for.

All of us who follow the essentially inane calling of putting dots on paper need finally and principally to face this inexplicable phenomenon of music; the fact that the known language of music means more than the unknown; that originality within an existing convention is more problematical and less spectacular than novelty; that it is more difficult to write 'easy' music than it is to write 'difficult'; that the Emperor's New Clothes is in fact a true story.

Perhaps it is something to do with honesty of expression; that instinctive impulse to grab, magpie-fashion, at the sweet that most appeals to you, oblivious to What People Will Say.

and onwards back to Manama itself, an enormous crescent around the entire top of the island.

Perhaps I wasn't clear in my own mind about what it was I was looking for. Some image of tranquillity, perhaps, where the people and the landscape worked in harmony together in a traditional way that would contrast with the frenetic land-grabbing opportunism of modern Bahrain. Perhaps I was fooling myself, over-romanticising, looking back towards a traditional way of life that may have been picturesque but was never as comfy as we would believe.

The section of *Salaams* that I had in mind was

Date picker

Consequently Fanshawe – largely out of naivety – grabs and clutches at every bit of the musical jigsaw. This is both the fault of his music and also its attraction. In *African Sanctus* and *Arabian Fantasy* he uses all sorts of techniques, from out-and-out Rock to Palestrina-style sixteenth century counterpoint. In *Saalams* he mixes moments of sublime musicality with manic, egotistical and embarrassing twittishness – at least to everybody else in the world apart from D. Fanshawe.

'The way I see it,' he said, 'is for me to do it to playback, so that I'm up a palm tree with a megaphone shouting '*Oomi-Oomi-Oomi*' and the camera sort of zeroes in on me, up the palm tree, dressed in traditional Arab clothes.'

'No, David.'

'It would be very beautiful.'

'No, David.'

'I could *pretend* to be shouting through a megaphone.'

'No, David.'

'And I'd look very dramatic in Arab dress and there would be these black-veiled women, the mothers, in a long line coming through the date gardens . . .'

'David,' I said, 'we shall keep your fat face right out of it. And instead we'll find a nice little palm garden and we'll get a can of petrol and set an old car tyre alight. Then, if the sun is strong enough breaking through the palm branches, the smoke will give the camera something to bite on. I can then take a number of differently angled shots up through the trees without you there at all. And when we cut them together we'll have exactly the same antiphonal effect visually that you've cooked up in the music.'

'Oh.'

We found our palm garden. It was not, admittedly, the innocently pastoral village I had imagined, for the extensive reclamation of land and the demand for water had upset the natural springs. The water-table, flooded with salt water, had reduced many acres of palm gardens to so many stunted spikes. Instead we found the ideal place where nature had undoubtedly benefited from the help of man and a government grant – in the Experimental Gardens at Budaia.

This did not worry me over much. The best and most convincing sequences in *African Sanctus* had been shot in the Botanical Gardens, Khartoum, where the lily pads and bull-rushes on the gold-fish pond

DATE PICKERS

had served, on a long-focus lens, as a tropical swamp in the south of Sudan. It had saved us endless sums on air-trips, overnight accommodation, penalty payments for the camera crew and so on. The sky-line of a rubbish tip just up the road in Omdurman, shot through filters day-for-night, had saved us a week's trip to Marra Mountains a thousand miles away to the west. So I had few feelings of guilt in settling for the Experimental Gardens of Budaia.

'In any case,' said Khalifa, 'if you wanted to be totally realistic, I should point out that when you come back to film in February there simply won't be any dates up the trees anyway. It's the wrong time of year.'

'Good. The back lighting and the smoke from the burning tyre will mask things nicely.'

We drove back to Issa Town, the setting sun burning behind us to the west over Saudi. It was the sort of sunset you never quite believe when it arrives through your letter box on a postcard. A palm tree obligingly swayed for us in the foreground in a ripple of wind and the sun plopped into the sea. Even then there was enough light in the sky, indigo and violet, to enable us to film. Especially, and with touching faith in the subtleties of new, faster film stock, when the fairy-lights came on outlining a distant minaret and the moon rose high in the sky behind us, round and white as a ping-pong ball.

'Ooh, it's a bit nice,' said Fanshawe, surveying the scene through the back window of the ministerial Mercedes. With Khalifa pointing out interesting things to us every inch of the way, we joined our first hint of a traffic jam in the late wintry afternoon. In the other cars drivers huddled and shivered and genuinely felt the cold. They seemed to go in for balaclavas, wearing ridiculous black plastic crash-helmets with ear muffs, like the man in the circus about to be shot out of a cannon. Fanshawe and I

being British, were in our shirt sleeves, and failed to understand why the locals were becoming restless.

Then we realised that our driver, who had been with us since dawn and who was sorely missing his afternoon nap, was feeling the cold even if we were not. All day we had driven around with the windows down. Our driver had been far too polite to point out to us that while such a thing was fine for two mad Englishman in search of a palm tree, it was simply not on for a Bahraini in the midst of winter. To us it had seemed like a reasonably hot May day in England. But then we had not suffered a howling draught across the back of our necks for the past twelve hours.

Khalifa suggested that we should be dropped off at Falcon Cinefoto studio, letting our driver get home before hypothermia and frostbite set in. We could, he told us, easily cadge a lift back to our hotel with one of his assistants.

'They're all so loaded, they have a new car every week. They're much richer than I am, better dressed and better fed. They have Rolls Royces and I have to make do with a clapped out old VW mini-van. There's no justice in this life and I blame it all on Mr Harold Wilson.'

Khalifa's assistant, who indeed had just taken delivery of his new toy – a snazzy, lime green Toyota coupé – switched on the ignition and engulfed the newly born trading precinct of Issa Town in a blaze of 4-track splendour.

He let in the clutch abruptly. With a squeal of tyres we shot off, the headlamps carving through the rows and rows of identical houses. Like a model town display in the Toy Department at Harrods, proving what a clever child can do with the construction kit he got for his birthday, the Issa Town housing development is an identi-kit of what architects feel people like to live in. Each house, with its colour-

TV aerial, is the spitting image of the next. Each doorway echoes another. Identical windows face each other across identical streets.

But whereas similar schemes and 'new towns' always suffer when planted in England in the middle of some field near a motorway, Issa Town somehow seems to work.

Visually, the place has a constantly changing character, depending on the time of day. Architecturally, the buildings have a clean-limbed simplicity. Every inch of stone and plaster is painted in the same terra-cotta which picks up the warm, pink glow of the late afternoon sun on the desert. At other times of day the arched doorways and deeply recessed windows slice the harsh glare of the sun and throw black, geometric shadows across the facades. The decorative plasterwork, like so much middle-eastern art, is frequently modelled on Koranic quotations; that indefinable moment when religious experience merges with calligraphy, like the manuscript of a Bach fugue; when the beauty of the penmanship itself becomes a form of art.

A triple-archway, ceremonial but not grandiose, proclaims the formal entrance to Issa Town. At dusk the floodlights come on and the triple-arch becomes three-dimensional. The intricate panels of carving and plaster-work take on new identities. Slim minarets are picked out in fairy-lights, topped by onion-domes tiled blue.

An enormous sports stadium is filled for every match; in Bahrain you whisper 'football' and the entire place packs up for the day. The Stadium, consequently, is the pride and joy of every Bahraini. The fact that Issa Town also contains an Olympic size swimming pool, a cinema, public library, secondary school, technical colleges for businesses, engineering and commercial training – all these are taken as a matter of course. The planners, the archi-

tects, the ruling family may regard Issa Town as an astonishing social achievement, an ambitious experiment that works; high quality, low priced housing for 35,000 Bahrainis. But on top of all that, when the design awards have been presented, when the visiting delegations have been shown around with pride and the last Fanta bottled tidied away in the traffic-free, custom-built, tree-lined shopping precinct, it's the football stadium that will still matter most of all. Throbbing, gasping, chanting, despairing, rejoicing. When a match is on, the stands are a patchwork of red and white check head-dresses, intense faces lost in concentration, cigarettes puffed nervously and worry beads chattering like cicadas. When Bahrain United wins, it's a cause for celebration. When it loses, it's treated like a national disaster.

The general knowledge of football and footballers is astonishing; not just of the local team, but of others in Spain, South America, Germany and England.

'Foolham very unlucky no win Cup Final.'

The lime-green Toyota coupé skidded to a halt outside the Gulf Hotel with a screech of brakes.

'Sorry,' I said, 'I'm not very well up on football.'

'Tommy Trinder all very good, but Foolham directors need to get more punch into the attack. Especially in mid-field.'

'How very true.'

'Also defence goes to pieces under pressure. Bye, bye.'

With a roar the Toyota swept off before my total ignorance became too obvious, the headlamps sweeping in an arc around the hotel forecourt, What possible explanation could I have for living in SW6 and knowing nothing whatsoever about my own local team?'

In the hotel lobby three messages awaited me when I collected my room key. All three said the same thing: Would Fanshawe and I care to lunch with Mr

The souk

Bill Giraf the following day?

'Is this one of your jokes?' I asked Fanshawe.

'Nothing to do with me, old chap. Honest.'

'Are you quite sure you don't know anybody called Giraf?'

'Positively. Might it be a code?'

In the middle of dinner the Head Waiter weaved over to our table past the hotel *vocaliste* in her gold lamé trouser suit and a group of young Bahrainis chatting up a brace of air-hostesses.

'Mr Bill Giraf for you sir, on the telephone.'

All would now be explained, I thought. But by the time I reached the phone the mysterious Mr Giraf had rung off.

His identity worried me and nagged me intermittently through the night. It nagged me over my Finnan Haddock at 0700. It nagged me at 0800 at the Helicopter Station and through the rest of the morning's recce in the Old Harbour at Muhurraq. For wherever we arrived a message awaited us. Sooner or later, there was little doubt, we should meet up with the ineffable Mr Bill Giraf, like Joseph Cotten encountering Orson Welles in *The Third Man*. Whoever he was, this Mr Giraf knew our movements before we did. He was watching us, but we couldn't see him. It was distinctly unnerving. We returned to the hotel for lunch.

'Oh, there you are at last! You'll have to move like greased lightning. Mustn't keep the Ambassador waiting!'

James Belgrave had been pacing up and down the lobby of the Gulf Hotel for half an hour. Large, brisk and in a hurry, he had no time now for formal introductions.

'Suit and tie job, I'm afraid. Can you make it in two minutes? It's steak and kidney!' he snapped.

'Yaroo!' said Fanshawe. We both highjacked the lift, returning in record time with neat partings, clean hankies and after-shave doing its best to eradicate the lingering traces of the morning's visit to Muhurraq Fish Market.

So this was the ubiquitous 'Mr Bill Giraf'; author of all the official guide-books, a fountain of information, infinitely knowledgeable consultant to numerous businesses, endlessly resourceful in all matters of protocol, Bahraini born but impeccably English, and – just like his father before him – very close to His Highness.

James's father, Sir Charles Belgrave, described by one author as 'tall, cool, cheroot-smoking, very, very efficient' had been adviser to the previous ruler

Sheikh Sulman. James has carried on that tradition of calm excellence. Between them father and son, in countless subtle ways, have nursed that part of the Middle East from its days as a minute British Protectorate, through one crisis and another, through its growing significance in the oil world up to the present self-governing status. Modern Bahrain, discreetly democratic and raring to go, owes a lot to the Belgraves.

'The Embassy car should be here at any moment,' said James, after he had driven us to his house. He stood on the front lawn, rocking gently on his heels, hands clasped behind his back just like the Duke of Edinburgh. I thought to ask him why the D. of E. and people like himself who were close to Royalty always seemed to clasp their hands behind their back, but, instead, I asked him why his lawn was the lushest and greenest in Bahrain.

'Have it flown in from Fortnum's once a week, old chap,' he replied. And, for all I know, he could well have been telling the truth, so effortlessly persuasive was his manner.

The Ambassador turned out to be a round and very jolly man who asked us to call him Jock. His Excellency possessed an outrageous fund of limericks and had an awfully nice wife who knew a man at Boosey and Hawkes.

We drank powerful gin-and-tonics from solid-bottomed tumblers like glass buckets. Fanshawe and Mrs Belgrave discussed their hepatitis. Then, like a mirage in the desert, partition doors were pulled aside and we settled down to Mrs Belgrave's Steak and Kidney, Colman's mustard, mashed potato and succulent gravy, followed by cream horns, oranges in cointreau, cheese and coffee. Fanshawe had three helpings of everything to compensate for his hepatitis and reeled off stories of all the other Fanshawes dotted around the globe in the Navy, the

Woman in the souk

Army and the Foreign Office.

The Ambassador had, until recently, been in Moscow and the conversation ranged quite naturally about Philby, Maclean and Burgess, etc. Diplomats, it suddenly struck me, talk about things just like musicians discuss wrong notes.

The Ambassador's limericks grew even more colourful and, as lunch wore on and the wine flowed, the ladies tended to bray a little and the one next to me talked a lot about her husband's desalination scheme. The houseboy came and went, bearing various silver dishes. Fanshawe, hands cupped to his mouth, did his *Muezzin* call very loudly and apologised for frightening the houseboy just when he was carrying a silver dish of mashed potato in one hand and a silver dish of *petit pois* in the other.

'Oh, don't worry about him,' roared James, 'he's a Buddhist and nothing scares *him*!'

'How's Bunty these days?' somebody asked.

'Gorne orf with that Corffee planter's gel who gort kicked out of Kenya.'

'Good Gord!'

'Bunty's wife was shattered. You can imagine. Absolutely shattered. What a brick that woman is. Absolute brick. Absolute brick.'

Fanshawe said he had to remember to get some incense for when he performed *Salaams* at the Royal Albert Hall. James Belgrave said, 'D'you know, I think I've still got your original sketch of *Salaams* in the loft somewhere. You drew it out, the whole plan of the piece, on lots of sheets of paper all stuck together. It was full of graphs and squiggles and fifteen feet long. You left it here, must be five or six years ago.'

He leapt from the lunch table and disappeared as the conversation selected various names from the diplomatic bag, generally sorting out the entire British Foreign Office. It was a world I knew nothing at all about; an astonishing world of influence and public-school eccentricity. I had only encountered that world on one previous occasion, and that too was with Fanshawe, in Cairo filming *African Sanctus*.

On that occasion we met Hugh Leach, First Secretary, probably a Double First, brilliant brain, endless knowledge of Arabia, wise, eccentric and a First Rate Chap; Graham Greene couldn't have invented a better one. Hugh drove us in his battered Land Rover over the bumpy Sakkhara road. In the space of a few hours he showed us the old and essential Egypt of the Pharaohs, scenes and locations that had changed really very little over five thousand years. He struck me as being rather a cut above the cocktail-party world of the F.O. for he tended to do odd things like climbing to the top of the Pyramid of Mycerinus at night to sit reading Matthew Arnold by the light of the moon.

He could play *Once in Royal David's City* on the trumpet and I accompanied him on his ancient harmonium, brought out for him from England in the diplomatic bag. Playing Christmas carols in a study in the shadow of the Pyramids of Giza is the stuff the FO's made of. It makes yer proud ter be British.

James Belgrave returned to the luncheon table. 'Couldn't find your wretched fifteen feet of music,' he said, 'but, d'you know, I *did* find the barbecue that we mislaid in the summer!'

Sheikh Esa, true to his promise, collected Fanshawe and I in his golden Mercedes from the Belgraves. Suffering from extreme cultural shock, and far too much steak and kidney, we were translated from the amiable Kensington patter of the luncheon table to the deafening silence of the desert.

Since I arrived in Bahrain I had been disappointed at the apparent ordinariness of the modern developments, the barren and rocky landscape, the lack of any real visual or filmic interest. As politely as possible I had made this known to Esa, and he had said he would prove me wrong.

It was Thursday afternoon and very few cars drove south along the same road, except for one or two families heading into the desert to camp for the weekend. But we soon left them far behind as Esa drove us farther and farther to the south, past the craggy central rocks of Jebel Dhukhan surmounted by the space-age tracking station, and into the flat plains of the desert and even beyond to the salt flats and the waters of the Gulf.

Laying out the mats in preparation for a festival

He said very little. Occasionally he would point out one feature or another, a rocky promontory where, as a child, he and his parents would come for picnics, or the colour of the afternoon light on the shallow valley of Ermaitheh.

He took us to old lodges and ruined palaces in the desert where his ancestors hunted gazelle with falcons and salukis. Then he drove us up on to a rocky plateau. To our right and left we could see both the western and eastern rim of the island. The place was totally deserted apart from one solitary oil-well and the donkey engine rhythmically throbbing.

The total arrogance of this piece of machinery, pulsing and slurping in the middle of nowhere, its horizontal jib see-sawing endlessly against the setting sun, pulled me up sharply. This was what modern Arabia was all about, not the *Lawrence of Arabia* images I had sought so unsuccessfully. My pre-conceptions of Bahrain, with Hollywood sand-dunes and cut-out camels, had little to do with reality. I had, in fact, been looking for totally the wrong thing.

Sheikh Esa switched off the engine. We got out of the Mercedes and a sudden gust nearly knocked us off our feet. The sound of the wind rushing across the desert mixed oddly with the relentless throb of the oil well silhouetted against the setting sun. If ever there was an end-titles shot, that was it.

'What's this place called?' I asked Esa.

'Pump 238.'

'Is that all?'

'Until it runs dry,' he laughed, and wrapped his head-dress across his face to keep out the cold wind whipping up the sand. The jib of the donkey-engine had the words 'OIL WELL' on the side, like 'desk' 'window' and 'door' in an infants' class room. A pool of black oil, perfect as a mirror, reflected the setting sun. I hurled a rock into the middle of the oil and the image shattered. All around us stretched a moon landscape and the level rays of the sunset emphasised each boulder and indentation.

'Found anything you like?' asked Esa.

'You bet!' I replied. 'It's not every day you get a 360 degree set to shoot in.'

On our drive back from the desert we stopped at a tiny oasis. 'This is my brother-in-law's,' said Esa, 'he comes here occasionally to see his sheep and his goats.'

A man came out and greeted us warmly with a great deal of fraternal hugging and handshaking. He led us to a rough enclosure consisting of a circle of thorn and brushwood. Inside were a cluster of new-born lambs, their wool ringed by the back-lighting of the setting sun. In *African Sanctus* I had waited two hours with my cameraman Peter Bartlett on the dusty Sakkhara Road south of Cairo for just such a shot, a flock of goats approaching us radiantly back-lit on a 200 mm lens.

'How do you get these lambs so white?' I asked.

Esa's brother-in-law laughed outrageously. 'My shepherd,' he said, 'pops them in the washing machine when he hears me drive up.'

Parked just around the corner behind the sheep fold I noticed a Cadillac waiting to whisk him out of the desert and back to his air-conditioned, centrally-heated palace in Rifaa the moment he tired of being a shepherd.

'You seem to have things nicely in proportion,' said Fanshawe. 'But you wait till we get oil out of the North Sea. I've got some relatives up there somewhere and, believe me, the Sheikhdoms of the McFanshawes will clean up, and that's a promise!'

Last Stop Victoria

THAT EVENING over dinner, Fanshawe, in one of his B-flat minor moods, said, 'D'you think I'll ever be rich?'

'Not a chance, Fatty.'

'God, you're a cynical bastard!'

'What do you want me to say?'

'I mean, d'you think I'll ever make it, writing music?'

'Depends what you want. If you want to be rich, you'll be rich. If you want to be a composer, you'll be a composer – and poor! Let's face it, I know a lot of composers. But I don't know too many *rich* composers.'

'What I mean is, why do I always seem to have to do it the *hard* way?'

'Oh, give over. Not all that self-pitying spaniel bit again, please!'

'If only I could just write your plain, average, straight-forward avant-garde stuff, I'd be made!'

'You're getting right up my nose again,' I said. 'Here am I – incidentally a much superior composer to you – devoting my not inconsiderable talents as a film-maker, to visualising your pathetic musical rubbish, and all you can do is whine about how badly done-by you are.'

'No. Seriously. D'you think my music's any good?'

'Of course I don't! It's a load of old codswallop. It wouldn't get anywhere at all if you didn't have me to visualise it, Peter Olliff to engineer the recording and Owain Arwel Hughes to conduct it in the first place. So get on with your soup and shut up!'

Even without looking I could feel his shoulders slump the other side of the table. The spaniel with the tearful eyes and floppy ears had returned. This time I had gone too far.

'If you'll excuse me,' he said, getting up from the table, 'I think I'll go and drop a line to Judith. I wrote her a post-card but didn't post it because there wasn't enough room left for the stamps. I'd forgotten how big these confounded Bahraini stamps actually are.'

'Sit down.'

'No, I'd rather . . .'

'Sit down. Talk. I'm sorry. I apologise.'

'No. It's not necessary, You're quite right. I'm not a terribly good composer.'

'You're just going through a bad patch.'

'I'm a failure. D'you know, when I met my wife Judith here she was working in the F.O. amongst a load of chinless wonders. And there was a particular boyfriend of hers – called Captain Hurricane. He used to sweep all the English birds off their feet and ram them off into the desert in a pink jeep. And when he heard that Judith and I had met just three times and got engaged, d'you know what he said?'

'Surprise me.'

'He said, "D'you seriously think of marrying him? For God's sake girl, go off and have an *affaire* with him, but surely don't *marry* him! Why the fellow's nothing but a ruddy *composer!*" '

'So?'

'Well, Judith and I *did* get engaged. And the following year we ended up in jail in Tanzania. See what I mean? I have to do things the hard way. If only I could write string quartets or straightforward good old British symphonies for the Cheltenham Festival.'

'What happened in Tanzania?'

'Well, Judith and I went off on this mad trek around East Africa. And I wanted to make tape recordings of some fabulous drums I'd heard of. We got to Muanza – without any papers or visas or anything – this was in '72, and I asked where I could find the Sukumu Drums. And we finished up in the most God awful mess. The moment I mentioned the

David Fanshawe

tribal drums everybody shut up like a clam. And that made me and Judith even more determined to find them and record them. Originally, the drums used to be on the shores of Lake Victoria. Each corner of the Lake was a separate kingdom. Messages were passed by these drums – war, threats, good news, bad news – you know the sort of thing.'

'Did you discover the drums?'

'Not at first. But we found this fanatical French-Canadian priest in a mission. He'd set up a sort of public museum for tourists in Tanzania. That, at least, was a starting point for Judith and me. It was a very dodgy area, don't forget. And to get into the interior was difficult. It was a border area, very disputable, and access to waterways equals power.'

'Yes. I understand that. But what happened about the drums?'

'Well, when I asked the police for permission, I was told that under no circumstances would I be allowed to record the drums. I had no permission from the Provincial Commissioner, no authorisation, nothing. Anyway they're ashamed of anything that hints of tribalism. So I ranted and raved. There was an angry scene and I stormed out of the police station

and drove eight miles back to the French-Canadian priest and asked him if he could find the drummers for me. You know, the actual drummers who knew the rhythms and so on. Well, they were scattered all around the shores of Lake Victoria, and the talking messages – the war-patterns, the visits, the festivals – were barely remembered by the museum staff. They weren't your actual British Museum, peak-capped variety, but a load of scruffy attendants. They didn't even have proper drum sticks. It was after all only a sort of outdoor museum; a sort of concrete cavern which contained the tribal drums and lots of ancestral relics of the Sukumu Tribe. *Fantastic.*'

A waiter came over to our table and asked if everything was alright and said, with deep apologies, that Fanshawe's *steak au poivre* wouldn't be very long now.

'So I climbed up aloft with my tape recorder and Judith kept cave down below, looking out for the cops. And everything was going along fine; me on top of this great concrete thing dangling my microphone and the drummers down below thudding out messages on those damn great talking drums, When, right enough, up drives this Land Rover from Muanza

69

and a Police Officer – very smart – gets out and asks Judith what the hell's going on. "Where's your papers? Who gave you permission?" and so on.'

'Your *steak au poivre*, monsieur,' said the waiter, interrupting David.

'So, I tell the drummers to keep bashing away and I'm stuck up there on top of this concrete thing with my tape recorder and Judith is chatting up this snazzy copper for all she's worth, trying to charm him and so on. Well, I managed to get twenty minutes of recording of the Sukumu drums. But even with Judith turning on the charm this copper becomes a bit nasty and puts on this General Amin voice and says, "Meester Fanshawe. No permeeshin. You both come back to Police Station Muanza in your car. I follow you in Land Rover".'

'Vegetables, monsieur?' David ignored the food and carried on with the story.

'And I said to Judith that we ought to let the policeman go first in the Land Rover. Then with luck she and I could lag behind in our little VW and make a bolt for it up a side track. But this copper wasn't having any of that. And he followed us all the way and Judith and I were put into two separate cells for four long days and five very long nights. We were both made to strip and all our possessions were removed. We had no food. My tapes had obviously gone for ever. No bedding. Nothing. Just a little window and a view of Lake Victoria. And, believe me, I was shit scared that that would be my last view of Lake Vic.

'I went absolutely bonkers; ranting and raving. But I was lucky; I at least had a cell to myself. Thank God because I was terrified they'd put me in the common cell where there were about forty real hard cases, most of them smashed up and bleeding from *panga* cuts and absolutely terrible wounds. But Judith had a really rough time. She was shoved in a cell with a white prostitute who had epileptic fits night and day. We'd only been married a very short time and, God knows, Judith took it very well.'

'Is your *steak au poivre* alright, monsieur?' David hadn't touched a mouthful.

'Well, as I say, after five nights of flies and horror and total bloody fear, they let us out. All we got, thankfully, was a right dressing-down from the Chief of Police – for we were clearly in the wrong, and it was a clear case of disobedience – and that was that. In fact, to be quite fair, the Manuza Police were very efficient and were only doing their job.'

'What happened to your recordings of the drums. Were they confiscated?'

'No. As a matter of fact – and those coppers were really on the ball – the tapes were returned to me in immaculate condition.'

'Monsieur, you 'ave not eaten your *steak au poivre*. Shall I warm it up for you?'

David waved the waiter away, carved off his first mouthful and raised it to his lips.

'The most ironical thing of all is I distinctly remember seeing at the bottom of the great concrete thing housing the drums, as the copper led Judith and I away, a neat little plaque saying "Presented by the Dartington Trust" and I'd been at Dartington Summer school only the year before, lecturing about the joys of collecting folk music!'

Fanshawe rocked with laughter, took a mouthful of steak, and spat it out instantly, coughing and spluttering.

'Ugh!' he squirmed, 'it's got pepper corns all over it!'

'But monsieur, you 'ave asked for *steak au poivre!*'

'Sorry. My fault. I thought it meant pears,' said David.

So he had three helpings of chocolate gateau instead.

'But, don't you see,' he went on, 'how much easier it would be if only I could write straightforward music. You know – without getting mixed up with all this folk, indigenous stuff. But I need to do it. I've got this ridiculous need to record things before the Twentieth Century stamps on everything. And it's no good waiting. If you're going to capture this music – in Africa, or here in the Middle East, or wherever – time is against you. Literally, every minute, some bit of traditional life or other is smothered by a bull-dozer, an air-strip, a government official with a brief case, or some local toady with a clip-board. Those pearl divers, if we don't get 'em this time, they'll be gone for ever.'

'But David,' I said, 'there's something in it for you. Let's face it. You don't just tape traditional music; you base your own compositions on it. And a lot of people hate you for mucking it about and poncing off perfectly innocent, unsophisticated and instinctive folk music. Doesn't it ever occur to you just to record the dances and songs and so on, and then leave it at that?'

'And shove it all in a museum, behind a glass case? Sterile, academic, lifeless? Like tigers caged up in a zoo? Not on your nelly! If I'm going to collect folk music, it's not to shove it in a filing cabinet. I'm going to go on and on and on using those actual "live" sounds combined with my own music. At least – even if they're on an LP – they have an atmosphere and a vitality and a validity that's streets ahead of any piece stuck inside a museum. And, in any case, if people don't like the way I add my own music and if they think I ruin the raw material, then all they have to do is go to the governments concerned and dig out my original, unadulterated recordings. Because, wherever I've recorded, whatever tribe in whatever country, I've always given a complete set of tapes to the Ministry. So there! But you know what happens to things donated to museums? They get stuffed! And they finish up with little plaques saying "A Gift from Dartington", or tourist traps like those phoney *bomas* of Kenya, where you can watch your officially approved Masai warriors with neatly brushed hair, or go on safari to see the Dingi-Dingi Dancers with blue Playtex bras, or chaps from the City doing Morris Dancing in Hampstead High Street. It's happening everywhere. I tell you, next time you come to Bahrain, you'll find your traditional pearl diver alright. But he'll be in a glass case!'

'Don't you see?' he said, 'there are some things you

can preserve; a drum, a flute, a traditional head-dress. You can easily rebuild a mosque, tidy it up, and smother it with plaster decoration until it's unrecognisable. But though you preserve objects, their validity, their souls have gone for ever. And for me it's not enough to notate on the back of an envelope the songs of the pearl divers – like Vaughan Williams, and Cecil Sharpe – so that Benjamin Britten or somebody can add tinkly little piano accompaniments for the Wigmore Hall. I want to see and record those bloody pearl divers *as they used to be.*'

Fanshawe pushed away the few remaining crumbs of his chocolate gateau and looked at his watch.

'How's the time going?' he asked, exhausted.

'One-thirty, A.M.'

The restaurant was deserted except for us and one sad, patient waiter having a quiet puff over by the bandstand, cupping the dog-end in the palm of his hand, the smoke curling up oddly behind his hip pocket.

'Come on, it's late,' I said, 'he's waiting to lock up.'

'No, I don't mean what *time* is it, but what *day* is it; Thursday?'

'Friday. The day of rest. Ask the front desk to give you a call at 5.30. I want to be down at the Fish Market before dawn.'

'But that's only three hours' sleep. Bloody slave driver!'

'Well you shouldn't have got stuck in that Muanza Jail for so long! Goodnight.'

MINARET

OLD AND NEW BAHRAIN

CARVED DOOR

SALUKI DOGS BY THE SEA SHORE

VEGETABLE MARKET

PLASTIC FLOWERS ON SALE IN THE SOUK

BOYS PLAYING FOOTBALL

DHOW BUILDER

Sequins for the
Albert Hall

'IT'S NOT the smell of fish that turns me over,' said Fanshawe, yawning a few hours later, bleary-eyed in the dawn light, 'but the sight of that chicken over there, still flapping about and decapitated before my very eyes.'

'Well, at least you know it's fresh,' said Khalifa. He turned to me. 'Have you seen all you want to see?'

The glistening rows of newly-caught fish gazed up at us. All around fishermen hacked their catch into king-sized cutlets. Every fish seemed the size of a battleship and capable of feeding an entire hotel. Their colours, glistening silver, blue and red were a cameraman's dream. It was only their beady little fishy eyes that worried me, gazing after us as we walked through the market, like so many mother-of-pearl buttons.

'The Delmon Hotel is just around the corner,' said Khalifa hopefully. 'Don't you fancy a cup of coffee and some toast?'

We walked back through the souk. The little open-fronted shop on the corner, Mrs Beeton's delight, was packed floor to ceiling with numerous trays of brightly coloured spices, their fragrance so heavy that you almost fainted with the scent. The little shopkeeper his face wrinkled like a walnut, sat at the front of the shop, weighing out tiny measures of spices with little hand-scales like they have on top of the Old Bailey. In a Players Navy Cut tobacco tin he had a set of weights. I looked at one of them and saw it was a coin saying 'King George VI Emperor of India 1943. One Rupee.' In the next shop they were selling electronic pocket calculators.

'This really used to be *the* place,' said David as we entered the Delmon Hotel. 'When the British Navy were in Bahrain, the Delmon was where you went. It used to be a really swinging place with all the young sheikhs in their kaftans dancing with the English birds.'

The muzak in the Delmon Coffee Bar gave us *Tiptoe through the tulips, I'm for ever blowing bubbles* and *When Irish eyes are smiling* in that order, played on a banjo, recorded no doubt in Wardour Street, trying to sound like an *oude*.

'Dear oh dear,' said David, 'how things have changed!'

Finishing our coffee we fled back to the souk, into the labyrinth of open-fronted shops selling everything conceivable.

'Must remember,' said Fanshawe, 'to get some sequins!'

'To get some what?'

'Sequins. You know, those spangle things that you sew on frocks. Like they have on *Come Dancing* on the telly.'

'Good Lord, the bounder's gone native,' said Khalifa in his impeccable cockney.

'Give over,' said David unabashed, 'it's for the dancers in *Salaams* in the Albert Hall!'

We returned to the little man with the walnut face and the hand balance. With great seriousness and genuine dignity he weighed out one *tola* of sequins with his King George VI rupee, screwed them into a twist of brown paper and solemnly handed them over to Fanshawe.

'*Salaam aleikham*' said Fanshawe.

'Don't mention it!' said the little man with the walnut face.

Entranced by the whole Arabian Nights world of the souk, Fanshawe wandered in and out of one shop after another. The mixture of old and new was totally beguiling; hand-scales next to computers, women in *purdah* wearing black leather masks, bundles of shopping on their heads and digital watches on their wrists, donkey carts going one way and sleek young sheikhs in Ferrarris going the other. Fanshawe, wandering amongst it all, like a man in

The fish market

The souk

a coma, would have bought up the entire souk and taken it to the Albert Hall.

'Must get some of those funny tubes with knobbles on the end that they use in hubble-bubble pipes,' said David, diving off down another alley. 'Ideal for dancers. They can wave them around above their heads like those Egyptian birds you got to do that stick dance in *Sanctus* behind the Sphinx.'

'How's about a nice pair of *wazars*?' said Khalifa, holding up an enormous pair of white cotton pantaloons.

'So *that's* a wazar!' I said. 'Now I know what the hotel laundry list is all about.'

'You wear it under your *thobe*,' said Khalifa, 'that's the kaftan bit. On your head you wear one of these little lace skull-caps. On top of that goes your white or red-checked head-dress – your *guttra*. And on top of that sits your *agal*, which is a woollen ring made like a rope. Very handy for tying up your camel to the parking meter!'

The little man with the walnut face caught up with us and asked David if he was sure he had enough sequins.

'Seriously,' said Khalifa, 'in the desert they used to hobble their camels with the *agal*. That's how it originated, with the bedouin. I mean, you couldn't have your camel pottering off across the Sahara every time you got off to do a wee-wee against a palm tree, could you?'

Fanshawe disappeared inside an open-fronted hardware shop, dressed all over with tin pots and pans, tin saucepans, tin plates and tin kettles, tin things everywhere from floor to ceiling like the flanks of a dinosaur. The hot sun clashed around us and the entire facade of the shop sizzled like cymbals.

Fanshawe reappeared with the only items in the shop not made of tin; an armful of candy-striped box-wood tubes loosely tied together with a piece of string.

'You see,' he yelled gleefully, 'they've got bobbles on the end.'

'Now you can always go into the hubble-bubble business,' said Khalifa.

'The Namarettes will have a ball waving these around in the Albert Hall,' said David.

'It'll be like Wilson, Keppel and Betty doing a sand dance!' I added.

'You can laugh . . .' said Fanshawe.

The souk

But by then the string had come untied around the hubble-bubble tubes and Fanshawe was on his knees in the middle of the one-way system outside the Delmon Hotel retrieving his bits and pieces amongst the feet of a donkey and the wheels of carts and taxis. Khalifa and I walked on towards the Harbour pretending David was nothing to do with us.

'Isn't that bloody typical?' yelled Fanshawe. 'Everything happens to me outside the Delmon Hotel . . .'

He came puffing up behind us, trailing pieces of string and bits of hubble-bubble.

' . . . It was there on that very spot that I proposed to my wife in her Mini. I'd met her for the very first time here in Bahrain only a few days before. And I took her to lunch in the Delmon Hotel and then, when we got into her Mini I said; "D'you know, I think we get on rather well together. D'you mind if we go off into the souk and buy an engagement ring?" And we went into a little jeweller's and she chose the cheapest ring in the shop. A single Bahrain pearl on a gold band.'

'Ah!' said Khalifa. 'Wasn't that lovely.'

'David Fanshawe – the Mary Poppins of Bahrain!'

'Unromantic sods!'

All the Way from Dover Docks

IN THE harbour the dhows creaked and wheezed in the sunshine. Being Friday the jetty had a rather placid air about it. One or two loads of cargo were being manhandled precariously across gangplanks, but nobody felt like work that day. Occasionally one saw little groups squatting on deck preparing lunch, cooking over an open fire a mixture of rice and fish. Another sailor, crouched in the little wooden box that projected over the water high up in the stern of the boat, was just squatting. Or was he? There was an unmistakable plop and an ever-widening penumbra of ripples spread out across the mirror of water. With a sigh of success he smoothed down his kaftan and climbed back on the deck, and another sailor was waiting to make use of the oldest and most efficient form of air-conditioning in the world.

'Wouldn't like to be took short up there in a force-eight gale,' I said.

'Better to be the fellow up there than the fellow beneath,' said David.

'Well, you know what they say,' added Khalifa. 'If you gotta go you gotta go.'

'That's the sort of dhow I came down the Gulf in,' said Fanshawe, 'when I was on holiday from the Royal College of Music. I hitch-hiked all the way from Dover, across Europe, down through Turkey, canoed along the Euphrates to Basra, and then through the marsh Arabs to Kuwait. Then finally from Kuwait to here in Manama Harbour for three quid on an open dhow. Nobody else on board spoke any English. Hardly surprising, because all the other passengers were camels, goats and dates. We lived off yellow rice. It was high summer in 1968; steamy and very hot. When I arrived here in Manama the water was completely still like it is today. Bright turquoise.'

A few hundred yards away a black wild duck suddenly popped its head into the water and disappeared entirely beneath the surface.

'That's a *loha*,' said Khalifa. 'They can stay under for ages.'

After what seemed an eternity the bird reappeared, stood bolt upright on the surface flexing its wings, then flapped frantically across the water until it eventually took off like an old Wellington bomber trundling along a runway. We walked back along the quay picking our way over a cargo of date stones that had burst out of their sacks, past crates with sides stencilled 'This side up' pointing sideways. Had it not been for the Sinbad-the-Sailor design of the dhows, with their huge teak prows, the harbour could equally be in Devon or Cornwall, for there was no sign of a crane or a fork-lift truck. Seafaring, I thought, is so elemental it minimises the differences between people. Then I looked up at another sailor squatting in the stern and remembered that at Henley yachtsmen go in more for the *Porta-Potty*.

'Rule Britannia,' said David, saluting smartly. And we climbed back into Khalifa's VW minibus and headed for *HMS Jufair*, once the land-base of the British Navy when David's uncle, Commodore Tom Fanshawe ruled the waves East of Suez.

'His official title was "Commander, Naval Forces, Gulf",' said David, 'and when he was in charge, my god, you jolly well kept on your toes. No messing!'

As we drove south through the Manama David built up a convincing picture of the British Navy as she was. The sea-dogs, the spit-and-polish, the endless cocktail parties, bridge parties, gossip and intrigue amongst the officers and their wives as they presided over an Empire that, actually, we'd already given away.

'The whole place used to sparkle with blanco

Weighing anchor on board a dhow

Cargo on board a dhow

Sailor on his dhow

Cargo on board a dhow

and Brasso,' said David. 'When the British were here it was one endless social whirl and you couldn't get out of bed in the morning without somebody saluting you and thrusting a gin and tonic in your hand.'

'Once the British moved out,' warned Khalifa, 'the naval base became, as you say, phased out.'

'There it is!' yelled David triumphantly as we rounded the last corner. And then I saw his expression change; he looked at the buildings as if he were looking at a kindly old labrador that had finally been put to sleep.

'Oh, no!' he said to himself very quietly. 'Oh, no!'

Khalifa switched off the ignition and we surveyed the rusty wire mesh fence, the tangled wisps of barbed wire, the paint flaking off breeze-block sheds, derelict, gaping, corrugated iron roofs, cracked windows and sagging doorways.

'But surely this used to be the main gate, didn't it?' said David uncomprehending. 'Surely there used to be sentries here, smartly dressed in white drill shorst with webbing belts and rifles with fixed bayonets?'

He got out, scuffing his feet across the pitted tarmac that was now nothing more than a muddy, wind-swept cul-de-sac, with a heap of rotting leaves, old newspapers and Coke tins piled against the barrier.

'They sprang to attention here as the officers' wives came back in the staff cars from the hairdresser or the Residency. They'd salute and say "Yes, sir! No, sir! Three bags full, sir?"'

Khalifa and I stayed inside the VW, watching David walk around in a daze like a survivor from an earthquake.

'It's horrible,' he said very quietly, 'horrible'.

'Let's try the other gate,' said Khalifa, backing up the VW. 'I think they use the other one these days.'

The other check-point was scarcely more im-pressive. Next to the hinged pole that served as a barrier, a couple of Beluchi soldiers in uniforms sat in the shade of the sentry box, having a quiet drag. They sat on those peculiar bent-wood chairs you only ever see lion-tamers using. A large sign in Arabic and English said Halt and No Admittance and various other things and Khalifa thought it prudent to park the VW out of sight round the corner.

'You'll never be allowed in without a permit,' he said. 'And the pistols in those holsters are loaded, by the way.'

'But I want to go inside and have a look around,' said David innocently. 'I'll just tell them my Uncle Tom used to be in charge here and I'm sure they'll understand.'

'David, David, things have changed,' said Khalifa. 'Please, don't make trouble.'

'Don't worry,' I said to Khalifa, 'leave it to me!'

I flashed my old BBC pass. In several languages, and with an impressive gold crest, it commands heathen tribes all around the world on pain of death to lie face downward in the mud and to grant the bearer 'toutes facilités dans l'exercice de ses fonc-tions'. Striding up to the checkpoint I barked several times and very angrily, 'Huwheldon! Huwheldon! Huwheldon!' straight in the faces of the guards. Like the Dervish in Omdurman and the Kikuyu thug in Nairobi – who had foolishly tried to obstruct the recce of *African Sanctus* – the guards cringed away in terror. For the BBC is powerful juju the world over, and – whatever the native language – the thrice-uttered curse of 'Huwheldon!' strikes terror in the heart of man and beast alike.

David thundered up behind me with a roar of 'FANSHAWE!'

This was altogether too much for the guards. Rudely awaken from their reverie they weren't at

David Fanshawe signs in at the base

David Fanshawe and Patrick Hamm outside the Commanding Officer's house, Bahrain naval base

all sure whether to shoot us or salute us. In the end one of them reached for a telephone, dialled a single number and said 'Fine. Showery'. At this, David took hold of the telephone himself and bellowed, 'My name is David Fanshawe with an E. My Uncle Tom used to be Commander here and he planted this tree, you see, and I'd like to have a look at that tree and see how it's getting on . . .'

As David rambled on I saw a bearded sailor in the distance the other side of the barrier, slowly and sedately cycling towards us on an extremely old bicycle. He had a beard and sat very upright on the bicycle and looked like Bob Hope doing an impersonation of Margaret Rutherford in *Blithe Spirit*.

Fanshawe was still pouring out his family history when the cyclist dismounted, said 'Hi!' and 'Howdee!' several times, introduced himself as Quartermaster Patrick Hamm and answered 'No problem' to everything we said. He was one of those totally charming, helpful and interested Americans one frequently meets in the most unlikely circumstances. He and David hit it off together perfectly.

'I hitch-hiked here first of all in 1967, all the way from Dover,' said David.

'Dover, *England*?' said Quartermaster Hamm.

'And I used to come here to stay with my Aunt and Uncle who lived just over there in Navy House. . . .'

Patrick Hamm was the perfect audience for Fanshawe. They made an ideal two-shot for a hand-held walk, with the camera following them at knee height, David chattering away about the Raj and the Quartermaster cycling sedately beside him.

They searched around the base for Uncle Tom's garden.

'He planted a tree, you know,' said David.

'Sure. The English do that a lot – plant a tree.'

I expected a statuesque oak, or at least an English willow. But although we managed to find the garden, it was quite difficult to find the tree, for it was rather small and somewhat stunted.

'Hardly Sherwood Forest,' said the Quartermaster.

'Get on with you,' said David, patting the thing affectionately, although its trunk was no thicker than a broomstick. 'It used to have a little plaque here somewhere, saying: "This tree was planted by Commodore Tom Fanshawe," and I think we made it an excuse for another party and cracked a bottle of

David Fanshawe and Patrick Hamm on the verandah of the Commanding Officer's house

DAVID FANSHAWE PLAYING THE PIANO ON THE PARADE GROUND

DRUMMER IN THE BAHRAIN POLICE BAND

DAVID FANSHAWE RECORDS THE POLICE BAND

champagne over it.'

'Maybe that's the reason it hasn't grown too well?'

'And over here, on the terrace, we had endless cocktail parties. There was enough gin and tonic on this verandah to float a battleship.'

In the ceiling above our heads three enormous Somerset Maugham fans were now still. But it was not difficult to picture the place as it has been only a few years before. Now, on that rather grey January day, the whole base was like a ghost town. From what I could tell, the Americans, like the British before them, had virtually pulled out retaining just enough staff to keep the place ticking over.

Now and again one or two casual yanks would saunter up in grubby khaki dungarees and baseball caps and say 'Howdee!' but they seemed more like warehousemen or motor mechanics than sailors.

At the back of Navy House and beyond the garden and the deserted swimming pool, we came to a wire mesh boundary fence.

'See that wire?' said David. 'When I came here first in 1967, that wire was the limit of my existence. I'd hitch-hiked all the way here simply to record the songs of the pearl divers. But British personnel were confined to base and so I'd stand here for days staring at this wire and the open sea beyond.'

A few inches away from the wire fence the water lapped gently, rocking the rushes slowly to and fro, The water, flat and smooth for miles, stretched across to the old quarter of Muhurraq and the pearl divers' beach, the beach that in those days had been 'out of bounds'.

'It was unbearably frustrating,' said David, as we waved goodbye to Patrick Hamm after thanking him for showing us around. 'I'd come all this way from England to Arabia, and for what? To stare, at a wire mesh fence!'

Patrick Hamm said, 'Too bad' and told us we would be most welcome to come back with a film crew. He climbed back on his bicycle, tinkled the bell and said: 'No problem.'

'Finally,' said David, 'I bribed a taxi-driver to let me stow away one night in the back of his cab. I lay there in the boot as the taxi drove out of the base and past the sentry guards. I slept all night on the pearl divers' beach under one of their dhows. In the morning, like Sinbad, I would creep out to sea with them and tape-record their songs. I don't think I slept a wink all night. Frankly, it suddenly struck me, I was being outrageously stupid. I was on a forbidden beach. Nobody at Navy House – not my Uncle Tom, nor my relatives, nobody – had any idea where I was or even that I was missing. I could have been robbed, stabbed, drowned, murdered for all they knew. I'd never stopped to consider the dangers. All I wanted to do was to get out there amongst the pearl divers.'

'What happened?'

'Well, at dawn, I was picked up by a British Naval Police Land Rover and taken to the white-washed fort at Manama, which was the headquarters then of the military police. There I was questioned by an irate, red-headed, English policeman. I can tell you he gave me a right bollocking! He was furious! There was I, a blithering idiot and nothing but an infernal nuisance, the nephew of the Commanding Officer mark you, and an embarrassment to everybody, breaking every rule in the book, and – can you believe it? – not only going into the native quarter, but actually *wanting* to mix with, talk to, listen to, be friends with people regarded by the British as hostile.'

'And *were* they hostile?'

'Not as far as I know! I think the reason for the "out-of-bounds" thing was that a bunch of Irish Rangers stationed at Hamallah Camp had gone off on

the booze one night, got a bit frisky hoping to pick up a couple of local birds who didn't want to know, and then got thumped when they refused to piss off. And, from what I remember of the Irish Rangers when I was here, they were a right little mob of rough-necks and deserved all they got.'

'But what happened to you, at the Police Fort.'

'Well, this ginger-haired copper had a go at me and said: "You come here to Bahrain, stinking like a shrimp boat, an embarrassment to every Englishman on the island, and what the hell d'you think you're playing at, you little squit?" And in front of him in that office was a huge glass-topped desk with a map of Bahrain and the Arabian Gulf. All the places I longed to go to. And I said to him, "You can jolly well get your men to take me back to that pearl divers' beach in the Land Rover ,because I'm going to photograph and record those divers whether you like it or not and you'll bloody well take me straight back there." And he said to me, "What d'you think this is, a ruddy taxi service?"'

'Did you get your photographs?'

'A few. Not very good. They drove me back to the beach and stood guard over me, almost tying me on a lead to the Land Rover. But by then the light had

gone and so had the pearl divers. What was worse of course was that I still had to face Uncle Tom. You can imagine, he wasn't merely angry; as my uncle, he was really upset that I had so wilfully disobeyed him. You can imagine, it caused endless gossip amongst the officers' wives sipping their pink gins around the swimming pool. The truth of it was, I, David Fanshawe, was an embarrassment! I mean, who ever heard of anything so incomprehensible and ridiculous as somebody wanting to get mixed up with *pearl divers*? The whole thing was totally outside their understanding. Their life was back there, around the swimming pool and their horizon stretched no further than drinks on the verandah and cucumber sandwiches and Earl Grey tea in my uncle's garden. How could they possibly understand?'

Fanshawe, I found out later, had then gone down with jaundice, and had spent a month in the RAF Hospital in Bahrain before being flown home by the British, no doubt with a sigh of immense relief.

'But before I went back to London – where, incidentally I was ill for nine months – I went to see the Ruler. And the great irony of it all was that *he* was the first person who was prepared to listen to me; none of the English had wanted to know. The Ruler gave me a gold watch and said, "Why don't you return? Come back next year and I'll see that you get help to find the pearl divers and record their songs." And that's what I did, in '68, hitch-hiking all the way from Dover Docks, and I went straight to see the Ruler and said "Here I am again!" and, true to his word he sent me round to the Ministry and they gave me an envelope, and in that envelope were 300 dinars.'

'How generous!' said Khalifa.

'I agree, it wasn't the money that mattered, but, more important, the Ruler put me in contact with you, Khalifa!'

That year, with Khalifa's help, Fanshawe met a few pearl divers and had recorded them as best he could on his little cassette recorder from Boots the Chemist.

'It was hardly hi-fi, and the recordings were made on land, and not at sea where all the real excitement is. But I managed to use some of those original cassettes in *Salaams*. Actually the grotty sound quality, as if the microphone was wrapped up in an old army sock, gives it a weird and rather haunting quality, like a scratchy 78 record played on a wind-up gramophone, amazingly atmospheric. But,' he turned to Khalifa, 'the Ruler was right! When I first met him he said, "If you come three times to Bahrain you will be lucky." True enough, when I arrived here for the third time in December 1970, an amazing thing happened to me.

'It was Christmas Day and I arrived here – again, stinking like a wrestler's jock-strap – having sailed across the Indian Ocean in a dhow. I'd walked around Uganda, and along the Tana River (where I'd had my canoe capsized by a hippo) and when I reached Bahrain I came straight to Navy House. The place was deserted. My Uncle, I think, was on a course back in UK, or, more likely, had got wind of my arrival,

which wasn't that difficult, and made a bolt for it when he'd seen me on the horizon. Anyway, as there were none of my relatives on the Land Base, I got a fisherman to row me out to *HMS Eskimo* which was parked out in the bay. And I was duly piped aboard and you would have thought I was Admiral of the Fleet and not some rotten old tramp. The first person I saw as I got on board was my cousin, Peter Moss, who was a Lieutenant.'

'You bloody Fanshawes get everywhere, don't you!' I said.

'Shut up and listen! Peter's jaw dropped a couple of notches and he took one look at me being piped aboard in my baggy shorts and said: "Good Lord, you can't come in here; you're not even wearing a tie! And, anyway, you're too late for Christmas Dinner, old chap. Pity. Still. Never mind, eh?"'

'But by that time they were lumbered with me and sort of had to put up with me staying aboard *HMS Eskimo*. It was all frightfully formal. Hey!' he yelled at Khalifa suddenly, 'There's Bung. 4-C.'

The VW stopped outside an undistinguished cluster of pre-fabricated bungalows.

'That was where I met Judith for the first time . . .'

'So, OK Holofernes; shoot!' It was getting near lunch time and I wished Fanshawe would shut up for a bit.

'She'd just come from the hair-dressers and was going off to a tennis party and I caught sight of her, a vision in a white dress, like Joan Hunter Dunne . . .'

'Oh, my gawd. Here we go,' and I started singing the nice big slushy tune from *Brief Encounter*. Fanshawe, totally oblivious, continued: 'I asked her if she'd like to invite me to tea inside her bungalow (she was in Bahrain working for the Foreign Office, at the time. Not so much a secretary, more a sort of spy, I reckon) and I sat on the floor at her feet while she handed me cucumber sandwiches and chocolate cake and I played her my piece called *Salaams* on my tape recorder . . .'

'*All* of it?'

'Naturally.'

'Jesus!'

'And, as she and I sat there together for the first time in Bung. 4-C listening to my music, you could have cut the atmosphere with a knife.'

'I bet!'

'And afterwards, when the tape was finished, she looked at me and said, "David," she said, "that was very beautiful".'

'Rubbish! She just wanted to get rid of you!'

'No. Seriously. She genuinely seemed to like my music and, obviously, was not only a most beautiful blonde, but a girl of great taste.'

'Dum-de-dum-de-dum-*dah* . . .' I had reached the soaring E-flat major bit of the Rachmaninov, where Celia Johnson gets a fly in her eye on Bagshot station, or was it East Grinstead? – and Trevor Howard whips it out with the corner of his hankie and they live happily ever after.

'And I said to her, "I must see you again," and she said, "But my boyfriend Captain Hurricane . . ."'

'Captain *What*?'

'Captain Hurricane!'

'You're not serious . . .'

'He was called Captain Hurricane, and he used to screw all the English birds like crazy and thrash around the desert in a pink jeep like Rudolf Valentino. And she had this other boyfriend called Stackpole . . .'

'And what did Stackpole do?'

'He used to drop in for tea with Judith – literally – arranging army manoevres so that he'd come parachuting out of the sky and would land on her verandah like Batman, just as she was putting the kettle on.'

'Is that all?'

'He was also awfully good on water-skis.'

'I bet!'

'And when Stackpole and Captain Hurricane and all the Irish Rangers up at Hamallah Camp found out that there was this squitty little minstrel from the Royal College of Music with his baggy shorts chatting up the best bird on the island, they went bananas!'

'Natch,' said Khalifa.

'Seriously, those Irish Rangers were real thugs, a lot of them. Real toughies who would sort you out as soon as look at you. A great number of them finished up as S.A.S. or mercenaries. And they roughed me up several times. Honestly, it got so serious I had to phone up their boss, Colonel Carter, and ask him to make them lay off. And *he* knew they were out to get me, obviously, because he placed an armed guard, twenty-four hours a day, outside Judith's bungalow, with a sentry clumping up and down on the verandah, while Judith and I were inside . . .'

'Humming your hundred best tunes from *Salaams*?'

'Don't be rotten! It was all very touching and beautiful! I first met her, this vision in the tennis dress, on New Year's Eve 1970. She couldn't come out with me because she was going to a Navy Ball that night. But I stole a red rose from outside the Officers' Mess to give to her. And every evening I would creep up to the carport – that one over there! – and leave a love-letter on the seat of her white Mini.'

'Ah!'

'True! There were three of them dated, 1/1/71; 2/1/71; 3/1/71. And the next day I asked her to marry me. She said she needed time to think. And three days later I took her to lunch at the Delmon Hotel and bought her a ring in the souk and so we got engaged exactly a week after we met!'

'Fantastic!' said Khalifa. 'But today is Friday, and I promised my family I'd be home to have lunch with them.'

Danah

POOR KHALIFA. Almost since our arrival he had been with us from dawn to sunset it seemed, had driven us to dozens of different locations, had acted as interpreter, friend, guide, consultant; the complete Mr Fixit. At the same time he had his own photographic business to run and his own things to attend to. It was largely because of his help that Fanshawe and I had been able to cram so much into such a short time.

But however much he wanted to lunch with his family, I could not afford to let Khalifa out of my sight. We were booked on the flight to London early Sunday morning. We had just one day left, Saturday, in which to complete the recce, arrange a shooting schedule, write a script . . ! There was no way we could part with Khalifa, not even for lunch.

'Khalifa,' I said, 'why don't you ring up your wife Tina, and tell her to grab the kids just as they are and you all come and eat with *me*? We'll all have lunch at the Gulf Hotel.'

There were nine hundred very good reasons why it was impossible, but in due course Tina and the children all arrived at the Gulf Restaurant, which, being Friday, was full up with no hope of a table.

'You 'ave not booked, monsieur?' said the waiter, and he cast an agonised glance at four adults, and four children aged eleven, eight and six plus little Omar who was nine months old, standing up in his pram, straining at his safety harness, hungry and at any moment liable to tear the joint to pieces.

'I am sure you can find us a table sometime,' I said, '*if we wait!*' For everybody knows that the one infallible way to get service anywhere at any time is to screw up the system, smiling as you go, until you embarrass everyone into submission.

'Put Omar and his pram there,' I said, blocking the waiters' route in and out of the kitchen, 'he'll be out of your way.'

Omar made a grab for a passing *spaghetti bolognese*, burped, was sick, grinned messily and said 'Goo-goo-goo.'

It was at that moment that a table for eight suddenly appeared from nowhere and we all sat down to fish and chips and drank cokes out of litre-sized beer mugs, then piled into Khalifa's VW minibus for Danah's Farm.

'All the horses I've seen on the island so far are very disappointing,' I had, on several occasions, said to Khalifa. 'Where are all those fiery Arab stallions with the arched necks and flaring nostrils?

'You wait till you see Danah's horses! They are the sort you want to film.'

We drove out to the west of the island past Hamallah Camp.

'That's where the Irish Rangers debagged me,' said Fanshawe, 'after I'd nicked a rose from outside the Mess!'

'Serve you right.'

'And over there,' said Khalifa, pointing across a rock-hard plateau of baked mud, 'is Danah's.'

The VW swayed and shuddered across a rutted track. In the back seat the children were asleep. Omar was snoozing happily on Tina's lap, quietly dribbling over her pretty Laura Ashley print dress. We were in the middle of nowhere, it seemed, getting closer and closer to a modern Scandinavian-style bungalow, elegant and dramatic with varnished pine ceilings cantilevered out over large picture windows.

We drove through wrought iron gates bearing an elaborate capital D. As we switched off the engine, the mini-bus was engulfed in an explosion of barking. A pack of salukis – aristocrats all and mad as hatters – yelped and wailed and snarled ferociously.

'What's the matter? You 'fraid they take leetle piece out o' your bom?'

Danah with an Arab horse

The voice was female, taunting, sparkling and unmistakably Swedish. Reacting like a TV commercial and with their honey-toned flanks shimmering in the sunlight, the salukis streaked out of the house, stood on their hind legs pawing at the low garden wall, and defied us to come any closer. Their pointed snouts were flecked with spittle. Their teeth were very white, I noticed, and probably designed for snapping gazelles in half. Like golden syrup they shone more than you thought possible. I don't know what shampoo they used, but they'd make *me* go out and buy it.

'Aw, come on!' Danah yelled above the din, 'Surely your not 'fraid o' my leetle poppies. They're all my babies, you cowardy custards!'

Danah, her boots on the table, rocked back with laughter. She got up from her chair on the verandah and walked out into the sun. She wore tatty blue jeans and an even tattier denim waistcoat. Her hair, the colour of straw, was pulled back by a rubber band into a sawn-off pony-tail. Her complexion, bronzed like a sherriff, with white squint-marks at the sides of her eyes, had seen a great deal of sunshine and no make-up for years and years and years. Perched on her head was a ridiculous pork-pie hat made of orange leatherette, pitted with playful toothmarks of innumerable salukis. Her hands were quite used to mucking out stables at 4.30 in the morning. Not occasionally, but every day of her life. Danah, herself a thoroughbred, was a knockout.

We left Tina in the VW. She was happily submerged beneath the four sleeping children who were all oblivious of the row the salukis were making.

'Come on in!' yelled Danah. Warily, we filed past her as she sat upon one dog, held two others in the crook of each arm and wedged open the fly-screen with one boot and the front door with the other.

'Hurry! They won't eat you! Isn't it terrible, I have to go through this palaver every time I want to come in or out of my own house. If the dogs get in there, they so playful they tear everything to shreds in ten seconds flat.'

Paintings and photographs of horses and dogs hung on the walls.

'See that mare? That's my old favourite, *Dahmeh*. Those paintings over there were used for a set of Bahrain stamps. But I don't much like; *Dahmeh* is prettier than that. She moves so beautifully.'

We sat around a long coffee table made of glazed tiles set in a teak frame. The room was spacious and well ordered. Danah, I guessed, spent less time there than she did in the stables. I told her about the film, especially about the section in David's LP entitled *Mizmar*.

'It's an Arabic word, I believe. Isn't it to do with horses?'

'You wanna film my horses? When?'

'In a few weeks' time.'

'Eeeempossible!'

It was the winter. Quite the wrong time of year. The horses' coats would be too long. Too short. Their eyes not dark-rimmed enough. Too fat. Too boney. She had no grooms. No trainers. No time. There were a thousand excuses.

'What a shame,' I said. 'We'll have to cheat and film it in England . . .'

'Cheat? Film Arab horses in Eeeengland? Eeeempossible!'

'It won't be that difficult. We can do it at my brother-in-law's farm in Buckinghamshire. His wife has some marvellous thoroughbreds. . . .'

Danah's ears perked up and her nostrils twitched, like a hunter on a frosty morning. There was a slight change of mood. At the risk of screwing up the whole thing, I played my trump card.

'Funny, isn't it,' I said, 'that if you want the best

David Fanshawe with an Arab horse

Arab horses you have to drive out of London down the A40 to find them. It's out past Fulmer, you know, where they do all that *dressage* and *haute école*. D'you happen to know,' I continued casually, 'if they still have those marvellous Lipizzaners there?'

'You know Fulmer?'

'Naturally. I learned to ride there.'

'You ride yourself? I didn't realise. Mmmmm.'

There was a pause. I hastily jumped in with as many horsey words as I could think of, talking airily about laminitis, cavessons, bran-mashes, hock-boots, snaffle-bits, curb-chains and running martingales. I had no idea what they were in Swedish or Arabic, nor, for that matter, in English. My total knowledge of the equestrian world derived from a few pony treks in permanent drizzle on Dartmoor, and a few agonising lessons at Fulmer being told to sit up straight and to keep my toes in and my heels down.

While we drank tea from Fortnums and David tucked into an orange-cake, I rapidly improvised a film montage to give her an idea of what was in my mind.

'Think of it as a sequence of close details,' I said. 'A nostril snorting. A flick of a mane. A huge close-up of a horse's eye. A hoof turning abruptly in the sand, and so on.'

'Mmm . . .'

'We could shoot it in slow motion,' said David.

'This orange cake's delicious. Can I have another piece? Scrummy!'

'Finish it off. My girl has never learned to cook, but she's dead keen and makes it up as she goes along. That's missionaries for you!'

There was a giggle in the kitchen.

'Sometimes she gets it wrong, but usually she invents something fantastic without realising it. Have you ever had kippers and cointreau?'

Fanshawe finished off the cake and we fought our way out of the house, past the salukis, carrying biscuits and Ribena for the children. A few Indian grooms and stable boys got out the horses one at a time and walked them around inside a corral made out of tubular scaffolding.

'Hi! Come to Momma,' said Danah, and an old but sweet-natured grey snuffled up to her. 'As you got a cold den?' And Danah wiped the horse's nose.

Dahmeh lengthened her stride and eased into a relaxed trot. 'You don't need slow motion cameras with *Dahmeh*. She's so beautiful she just moves that way in any case.'

The next horse, a bay, loped into the exercise ring. David, absentmindedly, tapped a rhythm with his fingers on the scaffolding fence. The bay frisked around a little and Danah said, 'You wanna see him dance?' She disappeared into the tack room and rummaged around. 'Just you watch 'eem go!' she yelled from inside and very quietly rattled an old battered tambourine.

The horse froze rigid for a couple of seconds. Then, with a massive snort, he reared up and exploded into a mad canter around the ring, twisting and bucking and generally showing off just for the hell of it.

'Did you train him to do this?' I asked.

'No! He does it naturally. He just likes to have a ball. All my horses react to something. This one likes tambourine. That one over there is keenky 'bout

plastic bags. You watch.'

The bay left the ring and the grooms looked anxiously at each other. They were small Indian lads; not very experienced. Gingerly, and keeping their distance as best they could, they led in a pure-bred stallion. His arched neck and flowing mane, and the precise bounciness of his stride, left you in no doubt that this fellow meant business.

'Now you'll see something!' said Danah.

The grooms slipped off his rope halter and scampered out of the ring like greased lightning. The horse was powerfully built and had a mean look. Like a contestant in a world title fight, the animal twitched his shoulders a couple of times, loosened up his muscles, waited for the bell.

Only it wasn't a bell, but the rustle of a plastic bag that Danah found, marked in the unmistakable green and gold of Harrods.

Like the previous horse, the stallion reacted instantly. But, with his sturdier build, each burst of speed was that much faster, each turn and twist and pirouette that much more dramatic, each glare of the eye and flick of the tail that much more menacing. Both David and I stepped back a couple of paces from the scaffolding perimeter as the stallion reared up above us, pawing at the sky.

'Steady, my baby!' said Danah. But the beast was having too good a work-out to take any notice. He redoubled his energy, thundering up and down and snorting in an uncontrollable frenzy.

'Steady my baby, or you'll snap something and hurt yourself.' Then, turning to us, Danah said, 'I think that's enough for now, don't you?'

'So long as you don't expect me to go in there and catch him!'

The stallion was now in full gallop. Only a landmine would stop it.

'Don't worry,' she said, ducking into the ring.

99

'I'll rugby-tackle it.' And that's what she did.

As the stallion thundered down towards her, Danah lunged at his fore-leg and just managed to touch it as it galloped past. The horse stopped instantly. The grooms pounced, slipping the rope halter over his head. Outside the ring they tethered him by a light chain around his fore-leg to an iron stake driven into the ground. Puffing, but completely docile, the stallion stood quietly, his flanks heaving like bellows.

'Some people think we hobble our horses, but that's not true. We put them on a chain, especially the stallions, and it teaches them fantastic discipline. They're perfectly happy and they get so used to the chain around their hoof that you have only to touch their leg and they behave. You see how easy it is.'

We drove in her Volvo Estate to her larger stables a few miles to the west, at Jezra. With total disregard for the deep pot-holes in the mud-track road, Danah drove in second gear all the way at a steady seventy. One tyre seemed to be almost completely flat. The car was but a few months old, and had only done a few thousand miles, but so severe was the punishment it received daily, that any other make of car would have shaken itself to bits long ago.

'Does it always make that noise when you drive over walls?' I asked her.

'Yeah! Kinda clonky noise. That's why I only drive over *leetle* walls.'

'You ought to be a test pilot. If this is how you drive a car, just think what you could do with a jumbo!'

The stable at Jezra held a motley collection of horses and foals of all shapes and sizes.

'This is a fair bunch of old coat-hangers,' I said, 'why don't you feed the poor things and put a bit of flesh on them?'

'In Europe you always keep your horses too fat. Arabian bloodstock doesn't have all that grass to blow them out.'

She explained how her mission in life was to re-instate much more selective breeding, to clarify the blood-lines and improve the stock.

'Over the years, you know, things can go to rack and ruin, and I'm weeding out the salukis as well while I'm at it.'

Just as I had done at the house, I told her how I would film the stables and worked out a two-camera set-up to cover the horses being let out in the early morning.

'See those two big gates there?' she said. 'After the grooms have fed the horses they let them out to graze on the plain. I tell you my horses all come out of those gates like you shot them from a catapult. But,' she warned, 'don't expect them to put on a show for your cameras. Remember horses are not people, and when they see you coming with your film crew, they may get a little wayward. You'll have the same problem filming my salukis.'

'Did you say filming your salukis?'

'But of course! If you film my horses, you'd better film my dogs or they'll get jealous!'

'Naturally.'

'And thank you,' said David, 'for the orange cake.'

'And Omar's black-currant juice,' said Khalifa.

And, I thought to myself, for the endless hours of grooming, brushing, combing and polishing you'll be doing over the next few weeks.

We all waved like mad out of the back, as the minibus rocked and swayed across the rutted plain. Through the window I could see her on the sky-line. Her orange hat finally dipped like the sun beneath the horizon as she disappeared in the clouds of dust we left behind us hanging in the still air.

Danah, we decided, was quite a lady.

Granny in the Works

WITH ONLY twenty-four hours remaining, the rest of our recce involved making lists for Khalifa. Lists of things still incomplete, people we'd failed to contact, locations I knew existed but which I hadn't had tim to find. I worked through the night mapping out a provisional shooting script and working schedule, so that Khalifa could complete arrangements in our absence. It was riddled with question-marks. But at least it was something to go on, even if – as would surely happen – every date, location and set-up got changed a dozen times. It tried to take into account the usual imponderables, so, inevitably a degree of clairvoyance was needed. You can, with common sense, economise on crew-hours by cutting down travelling time between locations, anticipate that Omani cameldrivers might turn up a week late or not at all, that the wind will change and your plans for helicopter shots have to be scrapped that day. You can also assume that one or other of the crew will, at some stage, go down with Khartoum Zoom or Delhi Belly. The question is, When?

Consequently the schedule contained some curious 'either/or' contingency plans: *AM.Aerial shots; Satellite Tracking Station, OR War Dance; Steps of Palace (if wet)*.

'There's still a big question-mark hanging over the pearl divers sequence,' said Khalifa, seeing us off at the Airport. 'But in the next couple of weeks I'll do what I can.'

The plane was packed with a weird collection of passengers. Businessmen, who obviously did the journey dozens of times each year, tapped out fortunes in the palms of their hands, then put away their little electronic calculators in slim brief-cases with locks like rat-traps. Fanshawe nobbled the window seat. I sat next to him and a black veiled old lady settled hesitantly in the seat to my right.

Like most Arab women of her generation, she was dressed head-to-toe in black, the only visible feature being an occasional glimpse of her proud, gnarled face. She had obviously never been in an aeroplane before, and got into a muddle with her seat belt.

We taxied on to the runway and the air hostesses performed the ritual *Dance of the Inflatable Life Preserver*, and the *Mime of the Oxygen Mask*. The old black Granny rummaged around in her white plastic airline bag and took out a gleaming stainless-steel Thermos with a teak handle. One by one, she produced tiny cups without handles in rich blue china patterned in gold, the size of egg cups, and passed around sweet mint tea to all and sundry in neighbouring seats. As soon as the 'Fasten Seat Belts' light went out, she moved along the rows, nodding and smiling but never speaking a word handing out mint tea.

It was interesting to note people's reactions; a British lady wearing gloves and a fierce hat, shepherding her twin grey-flannelled sons back to boarding school, winced with embarrassment, but was too polite to refuse. She sipped the cup, hating the sweetness, but each time she handed back the empty cup, Granny filled it up again and handed it back. The stewardesses tried to get past with the duty free trolley, but Granny was blocking the gangway with her inexhaustible Thermos. Being a Granny and a kindly soul she joined in lending a helping hand to the air hostesses, handing out whisky-and-gingers from the trolley as well as mint tea from her Thermos. When food had been served, Granny went round collecting up the dirty trays.

After a while a man in a peaked cap and white short-sleeved shirt emerged from the flight deck on his way to the galley. Granny handed him the pile of trays, cups and plastic dishes of half-eaten airline food she had collected. The man –

possibly the Navigator or Co-Pilot? – had never had this happen to him before and was furious at being mistaken for a mere Steward.

In the end Granny headed towards the First Class compartment with her thermos and handful of little blue cups. The rest of the VC10 needed a cup of tea. After all, being a Granny, she liked to do things properly.

Eventually she returned, settled in her seat and dozed off. The entire cabin staff heaved a sigh of relief. Airline routine has no place for traditional courtesy. Get a Granny in your works and who knows what'll happen?

As she snoozed in the seat next to me, the thin black veil slipped a little to one side and I saw her face for the first time. She had negro aspects in her features, possibly relics of the slave trade with East Africa; Lamu or Somali perhaps. But the quiet, Bedou movements of the hands, when passing around the tea cups, had suggested the desert.

There was a stir up at the front of the plane, and admiring glances were directed towards the elegant young woman emerging from the First Class compartment. She wore a beautifully cut brown velvet suit and a cashmere polo neck. The handbag and the shoes and her air of total confidence suggested money and lots of it. The woman was Arabic but her clothes and jewellery came from Paris, Rome or Geneva. She stopped when she reached our row, tapped Granny lightly on the shoulder and chattered to her in Arabic. Turning to go back to the First Class, she said to me in perfect English, 'Thank you for looking after my mother. I hope she hasn't been any trouble. They double-booked us up the front and this was the only seat left on the plane.'

The Granny fished around again in her white plastic airline satchel and came out with a brown paper bag containing a stick of Pink Glow lipstick, some green eyeshadow, some rouge, a yellow hair-brush (made in Taiwan) and an aerosol cologne spray with a mauve top. She graciously offered the aerosol to Fanshawe who smothered himself, getting an eyeful of the cologne by mistake and I had to lead David off the plane at Heathrow, his eyes streaming, and reeking of Yardley's *African Violets*.

On the tarmac the Granny was reunited with her elegant velvet-suited daughter, a cluster of equally beautiful grandchildren, and an entourage of nannies and chauffeurs. The family must have filled the entire First Class compartment and it's no wonder Granny travelled with us. She gently lifted her hand, wrapping her black shawl across her face to shield it from the wind sweeping across the airport. In doing so, her sleeve fell back, and for the first time I notice the Piaget watch on her wrist.

As Fanshawe and I stood there in the January drizzle waiting for the service shuttle-bus, the little Bedou Granny from the desert, together with her family and servants, was whisked away in what must surely have been the biggest black Mercedes in the world.

Russian Roulette in the Geriatric Ward

FOR THE next few weeks, while I worked on the shooting script in London and made final preparations for the filming, I kept an anxious watch on weather reports from Bahrain and long-range forecasts for the Gulf. The prospects were disastrous; 40 knot gales, constant rain and floods. As they say, if you're going on your holidays and you see a film crew, turn round and go somewhere else. For it is a well known fact that at the sight of a clapper board, the heavens open.

To make matters worse, it was an ashen-faced Fanshawe who turned up at the airport to fly to Bahrain with me and the crew. In a hoarse croak he said 'I've dot a told!' and, although he flew out with the rest of us, he went straight to bed with flu the moment we checked in at the Delmon Hotel. He stayed there, pumped full of Tetracyclin, sweating and groaning, for most of the first week.

Since the entire film consisted of exteriors, there was nothing to do but to sit tight and hope that the weather would clear up. In a way it's fortunate, if you're going to have bad weather, to have it at the start rather than at the end of your schedule when there are a host of other pressures to cope with.

'I rang the Met. man at the airport in Muhurraq,' said Peter Middleton, my cameraman, over his eighth round of toast in the snack bar.

'And . . . ?' I said, looking at the rain cascading down the windows.

'He said it's very rare that they have two inches of rain in the desert in February.'

'Especially in one day,' said Julia, our production secretary. 'Shall I order some more toast?'

'I think you'd better. It's going to be a long wait,' I said.

If you are a film crew you can expect to spend quite a lot of your working life in hotel coffee-shops eating toast and waiting for the sun to come out.

'I was once on a job in Ireland,' said John Hayes, sound recordist, 'where the bill just for toast alone came to £26. And, as a matter of fact, we were only there for two days!'

'If it clears at all, there's a chance of a nice sunset, with all this cloud about. And we might be able to grab a few pretties,' said Bob McShane, assistant cameraman, 'provided you don't want to intercut them with any sunny stuff.'

'I hate shooting off rolls of wallpaper, just for the sake of doing something. It's costly on footage and if the light's not right, it's liable to be flat as a pancake. Better to sit tight and have some more toast.'

We sat through several working days. With Fanshawe groaning upstairs with a temperature of 103 and torrential rain ruling out any idea of shooting, morale was sinking. Already, I had shown the crew the various locations scheduled. But what had looked sunny, reasonably romantic and exotic during the recce, was depressing and bleak in the foul weather.

After a few hours the rain stopped and the skies brightened a fraction. In the main street outside the Delmon Hotel, people started to reappear, picking their way around the puddles, hitching up their traditional Arab robes unaccustomed to the muddiness. Much of the souk was still flooded and gangs of workmen armed with brooms did their best to force the surface water into already over-taxed drains. The workmen worked shoulder to shoulder, broadside down the street, sweeping a tidal wave before them. From the coffee bar of the Delmon Hotel it was possible to see in both directions and to enjoy the total chaos as two gangs, oblivious of each other's existence, met face to face on the corner just outside our window.

But day by day the weather improved and tomorrow, the Met. man said, might be dry.

I looked at the calendar. It said Friday 13th. We had scheduled four or five different groups of traditional musicians to turn up for a bit of a hooly on their day off. Coaches had been arranged to collect them and to take them to an open space near Issa Town. Nearly all the musicians and dancers had negro blood in them, and the celebrations had originated in the New Year's Day jubilations when freed slaves and their descendants, dance in the streets in gratitude for their freedom.

Under lowering grey skies the charabancs rolled up one by one. We resisted the temptation to compensate for our week's inaction by shooting everything that moved, however much we felt like it. It was just as well; like so much folk music untrammelled by the restricted time-scales of gramophone records or public concerts, it all took quite a time to get going.

Fires were lit from dried palm-leaves. To heat up the drums and to get them in pitch, the women sat in a ring around the open fire, chattering away while the drum-skins tightened in the heat. A hobbyhorse dance started over in one corner. Behind us the snarling, moorish blare of a shawm cut through the nattering coach-loads, and a wizened little old man

Warming the drums

Pipe player

with cheeks hard as red billiard balls blared away behind us. It was a double-reed instrument demanding great lung-power. Like his slightly more sophisticated colleagues in white tie and tails playing the oboe in the London Symphony Orchestra, he possessed that death-defying ability to breath, apparently, through his ears, so consistent and uninterrupted was his phrasing.

Over his kaftan, like many of the men, he wore an old sports jacket. As he played he weaved and twisted, making figure-of-eight patterns in the air with the metal 'bell' of the instrument, patterned with brass rivets.

'If I'd known it was going to be like this I'd have brought ear-plugs,' yelled John Hayes, adjusting his head-phones and quickly turning down the volume control on his Nagra recorder. 'Look at him! The Leon Goossens of Bahrain! The snake charmer's friend! Go on whack! Get stuck in! You're bending the bloody needle on the tape recorder, and only Allah knows what you'll do to the Kirk O'Shotts Transmitter! But keep at it Abdul, little Johnnie's right with you!'

In addition to the large hand-drums, another percussionist clattered out an insistent 'three-against-two' rhythm with a couple of sticks on a battered oil can, held steady in front of him between the soles of his feet.

Like so much folk music, it tended to go on rather. In terms of cut-film it could sustain ninety seconds, maybe two minutes at the most of screen time. It possessed a hypnotic quality. In its natural state, the dancing would go on for hours and hours, getting better and better, until exhaustion won the day. But, for our purposes it was essential to be selective.

'I want two minutes of cut film, maximum, out of all this,' I shouted to Peter Middleton as he re-loaded

Women watching the musicians

the camera, changing magazines yet again. 'How much have we shot so far?'

'Seven rolls! Over an hour's worth!'

A shooting ratio of thirty to one; half an hour's film to be thrown out for every minute that actually appears on the screen. Too much!

'Maybe we should ease up just a little?' Julia yelled, clicking her stopwatch.

'You could always flog it to *World About Us*! They'd get a series of twenty-six episodes out of this mob!' Bob added.

The weather held. In the afternoon we set out for the Old Palace to film a war dance. The caretaker

Women watching the musicians

Warming the drums

Guard with Polaroid portrait of himself

slowly, and with such obvious good nature, that I instructed Peter to run the camera at 18 frames per second, to give the old men at least some spark of life when the film was eventually projected at the normal 24 fps.

'I've seen the Bude Bowling Club do better than this in a Friendly,' I said, 'and *don't point that thing at me!*'

Some of the oldest and most wizened war-dancers had turned up with ancient blunderbusses. The weapons were totally genuine, falling to pieces and utterly unreliable. The old men, it seemed, made their own gunpowder at home and kept it in tobacco tins in their pockets. Every now and again they would measure out a rough teaspoonful and ram it down the barrel. Then, to ignite it, they would break off the end of a match. As they pulled the trigger, the hammer of the gun might or might not set the thing off. You never could tell.

Sometimes it worked and sometimes not. The failures produced nothing more than a dull click. But the successes exploded with a sheet of flame and a bang that shook the tiles off the roof.

The art of it seemed to lie in knowing when to duck, and the afternoon developed into something like Russian Roulette in a geriatric ward. The old men, often sustaining severe powder burns, as if they had cut themselves shaving, roared with laughter each time they blew each other's heads off.

'They ought to take up this sort of thing down our street,' yelled Bob McShane, reloading the camera, 'Old Tyme Dancing at the Ealing Darby and Joan Club isn't a patch on this!'

The afternoon, consequently, developed its own momentum. The problem was not so much dodging the rain-clouds gathering above us as the muskets recoiling around our heads. Cameramen are used to working in dangerous situations; one week you

was a surly old fellow in an army greatcoat. The only trouble was, whoever ordered the bulk supply of government-surplus khaki greatcoats, had believed that the larger sizes would fit everybody and were the most sensible purchase. Consequently, although the caretaker was quite a little chap, his overcoat reached right down to the ground. He had an evil-looking and extremely mangy wolf-hound on a piece of string and we all kept well away from the brute.

The dancers were all men and quite old. So old, in fact, that when I organised them into a mad, frenzied mob storming the palace, they limped along so

The ritual war dance

The ritual war dance

Drummers

Bagpipe player

114

could be reporting a news story on an oil-rig
floundering in a tempest. The next week it could be a
guerrilla war the other side of the globe. Consequently, to survive in the hit-and-run world of documentary filming, a good cameraman will develop a
sixth sense and be aware at all times of the danger
around him. One eye will be glued to the view-
finder. But, simultaneously, the other eye will alert
him to potential hazards. Concentrating one hundred
percent on the smoothness of the shot, pulling focus,
anticipating the effect of the zoom and worrying
about the changing light and a dozen other technical
problems, is difficult enough. Walking backwards,
slowly and smoothly, operating a camera, is one thing.
But it is useful to know when you are about to step
off the edge of the cliff.

With several pounds of hardware on his shoulder,
Peter Middleton stalked through the dancers like a
panther.

'He learned that from Muncher,' said Bob, his
assistant, warding off the butt of a musket with the
clapper board.

'Who the hell's Muncher?'

'His cat back home. If you think Peter's good, you
should just watch Muncher.'

To shield Peter as much as possible from the
dancers leaping and barging around us, the rest of the
production unit formed a phalanx in a broad semi-
circle behind him, dodging out of shot and swatting
the musketeers with clip-boards and stopwatches.
Camera crews look extraordinarily silly from the
rear.

'Ready When You Are, Mr De Mille...'

FANSHAWE WAS furious that he'd had to miss the fun. With a raging temperature and confined to his hotel bed with flu, there was no alternative but for him to stay put and sweat it out.

'Couldn't I just come out with the crew tomorrow and watch?' he croaked, sitting up in bed that evening, his pyjamas soaked with perspiration. He looked like a Disney elephant who had been caught in the rain.

'This will keep you happy for a couple of hours,' said John Hayes. He handed David several boxes of sound tapes. 'I had to check through the tracks we recorded today, so I thought you might like to have these for your collection. They're copies of all the music we recorded.'

David's face lit up. It was the best present in the whole world and a very thoughtful gesture on John's part, involving him in considerable extra work.

'Whooppee!'

David leapt from his bed of pain and wound the first reel of tape on to his Stellavox. All that night the Delmon Hotel echoed to the throb of war drums and the crackle of musket fire. It was soon after that we moved to the Hilton.

With David back in action and the weather improving, our filming schedule looked more hopeful. At the old ruined Palace at Sakhir, in the middle of the desert, on a bright, windy day, we filmed to playback two traditional instruments – a *tabla* player and a *kanoun*. Both instrumentalists proved to be superb players, able to memorise very quickly elaborate rhythmic patters and musical phrases, and to mime accurately as we played them David's recordings already mixed with western instruments.

The Sakhir Palace I always felt, would be a cameraman's dream with its 'Arabian Nights' archways and the flat expanse of desert in the background. The harsh afternoon sun carved deep shadows in the flaking stonework and there was just enough breeze to ruffle the head-dresses of the musicians.

And at the end of the day, on our way back to the hotel, we were blessed with another bonus. On a narrow strip of sand, several hundred yards away from the road, three small boys were larking around on an old bicycle; one of them sitting on the handle-bar and the other two standing on the saddle and the rear mud-guard. Behind them the setting sun floated in the sky like a large orange football. Stretching horizontally behind the children was a narrow strip of water, the wind rippling the surface in a dazzling ribbon of light, silhouetting the moving figures with a soft rim of gold. It was one of those freak coincidences of filming where the place, the light and the weather are all on your side. The total effect was magical.

'I think we might . . .' I suggested. But already we had slowed to a halt and Bob McShane was screwing on the telephoto lens and Robin Constable was getting out of the van with half a dozen Hassel-blads swinging from his neck.

Although we moved as unobtrusively as possible, the children spotted us and, naturally curious, were heading our way. The whole thing was ruined.

'What time Concorde come?' I asked them and gazed up into the sky in the opposite direction. They giggled at each other.

'You too early mister. Concorde come in three weeks time for maiden flight.'

They roared with laughter as we set up the camera and tripod, pointing the telephoto lens away behind us in the vague direction of Muhurraq Airport.

'You three weeks too early, Mister!'

After a while the children got bored. The entire film crew stood there gesticulating at the empty sky until, eventually, the kids moved off. With many queer looks and much tapping of their heads

Musician with Kanoun

at our foolishness, the children lost interest and went back to play with their bicycle. While we stood gazing in the opposite direction, Peter casually swung the camera around 180 degrees and pointed the front of the lens through the crook of my arm, shooting back at the figures on the bicycle.

'OK,' murmured Julia after a while, 'that's another in the can. Everybody back on the coach!'

With the weather apparently settled, at least for the next few days, I decided to re-schedule the helicopter filming. The *Shamaal*, still blowing from the north, combined with a possible recurrence of the torrential rain, could still play havoc with our plans. The wind had dropped a little each day; Saturday it was 21 knots, Sunday 19, then 15, and – by the middle of the week – a blustery 10 knots.

Major 'Pip' Travell, in charge of the helicopter station, struck you as being the sort of person who – should it have been necessary – could have won the Battle of Britain single handed. He greeted us warmly and, within seconds, was nattering away nineteen to the dozen with Peter and Bob, both of whom are flying fanatics. Pip, in bright orange flying suit and a Biggles-type leather flying helmet (and full of stories of the 'How do you find out who's the Irishman in a car-wash? He's the one on the motorbike!' variety) told us he had volunteered to join the Royal Aircraft Reserve six months before the 1939–45 War.

'Then, when the beastly War started, I volunteered to leave. But they wouldn't let me and shoved me into Flying Fortresses lumbering through the sky,' he told us. 'Got hit twice, dammit! Once by the Jerries. Once by a British Warship off the coast of Scotland.'

He explained that with four people aboard – cameraman plus assistant, Pip and myself – the helicopter could only carry twelve minutes' fuel.

'After that,' he mentioned, 'it's downhill all the way!'

While Fanshawe drove off with Khalifa to the first location – on top of one of the immense storage tanks at the BAPCO Oil Refinery – we flew towards the satellite tracking station with its huge reflector dish, seeking some aerial shots.

'Not terribly keen on flying actually directly *into* the beam,' yelled Pip on the intercom, 'supposed to do peculiar things to a chap's whatnots, and the boffins over in Cape Kennedy get their knickers in a twist thinking the Martians have landed!'

On our second sortie we headed for the Tank Farm. Crackling on the walkie-talkie, Khalifa informed us that David was at last in position on top of the largest of the storage tanks, but could we please hurry as he might fall through at any moment.

Even from a distance of a mile or more we could see Fanshawe behaving like a demented fly on a cake tin, leaping up and down on the dome of the largest oil storage tank. The sound of the helicopter made him act up more and more as we hovered in for a closer shot.

'Curious way you chaps earn a living,' said Pip. 'Say when you've had enough, because those are high-tension electricity pylons outside your window and, I hate to mention it, but the wind's changing. We've only got half a cupful of juice left.'

The helicopters and the military band, both housed in the same white-washed fort, happen to share the same barrack square. Regrettably, as we came in to land, the Highland Bagpipe Band of the Bahrain Police were somewhat oblivious of our arrival, marching and countermarching beneath us. When the Scots invented bagpipes, they did so to terrify their enemies, and, with so many decibels skirling across the parade ground, the band left it to the point of decapitation before breaking ranks, tucking up their kilts and rushing for cover.

DAVID FANSHAWE PLAYS ALUMINIUM DRUMS AT THE ALBA PLANT

DAVID FANSHAWE CONDUCTING THE TUG-BOATS

WANDERING FOLK MUSICIANS

PIPE PLAYER   BAGPIPE PLAYER WITH MUSICIANS   KANOUN PLAYER

The Kanoun

Colin Moore, the helicopter maintenance engineer, ducked beneath the main rotor blades and helped us out of our safety harness.

He gave a long, low whistle. 'Pushing your luck a little?' he said.

I looked at the fuel gauge. 'Does that thing tell the right time?' I asked.

'Spot on!'

'How much fuel did we have left?'

'At a rough guess, I'd say fifteen seconds.'

'Do you make a habit of that?'

'Pip tends to. I must remember to have a word with him about it.'

Over lunch Fanshawe said that the security man at the oil refinery had told him how lucky he'd been.

'What did he say?' I asked.

'Only that those oil-tanks I was bouncing on have been known to cave in. They're not designed for that sort of thing apparently.'

During the next few days we completed the rest of the sequence: David drumming pearl divers' rhythms on oil pipes, conducting foghorns with semaphore flags, and signalling to tankers moored in the bay. By the end of the week we had ticked off the majority of shots in the schedule and achieved the front page of the local paper.

But one enormous gap still remained: The pearl divers. Time and again Khalifa had promised us that he had organised everything, that one day soon he would assemble the divers, organise a pearling dhow and all would be well. But when?

'Next Friday,' he told me. 'But ...'

'But what?'

'But you will have to film them without me. I have to accompany His Highness to Paris and London to do the stills photos when The Ruler goes on the State visit and ...'

'But Khalifa. You are the only person on the island who can make sure the divers turn up.'

'It's OK. You'll have Ali to help you.'

'Who is Ali?'

'You can meet him tonight. I'll bring him round to the hotel.'

To lose Khalifa at that stage of the filming was very serious. All through the recce, the planning and, so far, through the actual filming, Khalifa had worked directly to me. Inevitably he and I had discussed at every stage all those numerous details that one carries mentally and never needs to write down, information about contacts, people, names, the way apparently unrelated shots would eventually be cut

David Fanshawe conducts the tug-boats

David Fanshawe plays the oil pipes

David Fanshawe records the sounds of the oil pipes

together, technical minutiae, and the thousand and one snags that were bound to occur during the rest of the filming and how we would cope with them.

'Don't worry,' said Khalifa that evening. 'I have briefed Ali. He can carry on instead of me and be with you to sort out any problems.'

I looked at Ali. True enough he looked capable of sorting out anybody. He was about five feet tall, five feet wide and built like a wrestler, which, indeed, he had once been.

'I can be with you all the time during the day,' he said. 'At the moment I'm on the Graveyard Shift!'

Roaring with laughter – something he did very frequently – he explained that he worked at nights as a security guard. With several rapid chopping motions of his hand, he said he was a karate expert and, swearing undying devotion to the film, would make mincemeat out of anybody who got in our way. In any case, apart from Ali – who weighed nearly twenty stone – we still had Saeed who weighed around six stone. Between the two of them, Khalifa assured me, all would come out right in the end. Both Ali and Saeed were thoroughly good chaps. Although he spoke no English, Saeed had a little pale-blue pick-up truck, an ear-to-ear grin and teeth that appeared to be made of tin. Ali was fat and very capable; Saeed was thin and quite silent. We may not have Khalifa any more, I thought, but at least we've got Laurel and Hardy.

When the appointed day arrived to film the divers I telephoned the ever-cheerful Aussie Met. Officer at the airport. It was 4.30 am and he talked at great length about Highs and Lows and Isobars which, at that time of day, was nice of him, but quite meaningless to me. Obviously his was a lonely life and he welcomed the chance of having somebody to talk to.

Without wishing to appear too crushing I interrupted his rolling Aussie voice just as he was beginning to wax eloquent about 'a bit of a trough over Saudi.'

'But will it be *sunny*,' I asked.

'If it's blue skies you're after, Sheila, you might be about as lucky as a pork pie at a Jewish wedding!'

Ali told me he had arranged for the pearl divers to be collected in Muhurraq. They would meet us beyond the palm gardens near the Alkhamis Mosque with the twin minarets.

How many divers would there be?

Ali was not too sure about that. But, he assured me, Khalifa had explained everything to Allun – the old, blind leader of the divers – and, since Allun had given his approval, the divers would meet us as arranged. For after all, some years back when the Walt Disney unit had been shooting in Bahrain, everything had been fixed via Allun. If the divers had turned up for Disney, the divers would turn up for us.

'There's one big difference,' I pointed out to Ali. 'Disney was over here some time ago, when pearl diving was still flourishing. Also, I believe, Disney paid out something like 250,000 dollars. Their unit spent twelve months here on the film, over two months on the recce alone and nearly three weeks on just the divers' sequence. We're not quite in that league, and if Khalifa has offered payment to the divers, you can rest assured it's nothing like as much money as Disney offered them.'

'Stop worrying,' said Ali. 'I'll get the divers to you and you can film away to your heart's content – just like it was Disney!'

Just like it was Disney.

As we drove to the meeting point, following Saeed's pick-up, my heart sank. I remembered the very first time I had discussed with Khalifa the way

David Fanshawe records the pearl divers on their bus

I wanted to film the divers. It would be the wrong time of year, he had said. It would be impossible to do it my way; the waters of the Gulf would be too cold for the divers to go to sea. In desperation, and purely as a joke, I had on that occasion said to Khalifa that if the worst came to the worst I would film the divers in the swimming pool at the Hilton, and he had virtually taken me at my word, and chosen the next best thing.

Saeed's duck-egg-blue truck bounced along the road in front of us. To my horror it turned off the main road and headed for the Adari Pool. It dawned on me that Khalifa, unable to persuade the divers to go to sea, had done what Disney had done: take the divers to a fresh-water public swimming pool and fake the sequence.

'Stop him!' I yelled. And although we hooted for all we were worth, it was impossible to stop Saeed's little blue lorry.

'Blast!'

It was bitterly disappointing to think that our film should be reduced to this; that the best we could do was to cheat up a sequence in an open-air public swimming pool. We might as well have stayed at home and done it with half a dozen extras in Ruislip Lido.

We stopped by the pool and Saeed jumped out of his little blue pick-up with the red wrought-iron railings along the side, and flashed his tin teeth at us.

'Water. Very good!' he leered.

I looked at my watch. Any moment now and Ali would arrive with one or two moth-eaten pearl divers. I looked at the crew and the crew looked at me.

'So,' said John, flicking a mosquito off his Nagra tape recorder, 'what d'you think of it so far?'

'Ruggish!' said Julia, organising the coffee.

'Dear Diary,' said Bob, unloading the tripod, 'we were promised all these butch arab sailors and . . .'

'Bonjour, matelot!' said Peter, 'my watch says 6.30 am. Shall we call it a day?'

'Can you keep your voices down?' said John, the other side of the pool. 'I'm trying to grab a buzz track. Just for old time's sake.'

Like the rest of the Bardic Film Unit – including the mysterious Hugh and Muncher the cat, back in London coping with the film 'rushes' – John our sound man was, from first to last, a total professional.

As things looked I had little need for a buzz track. At best it would be a few minutes atmos; apparent silence; the almost imperceptible rustle of a light breeze in the palm gardens. Should we, by any remote chance, ever get something to film in that particular location, a buzz track would be useful at the sound dubb to iron out the differences in sound quality between one shot and the next.

We all stood silent, except for Saeed, who got into his little blue lorry with the red wrought-iron railings and drove off to home, kids, breakfast and sanity.

'D'you mind!' yelled John from the palm gardens. 'When the lorry's disappeared, can you please give me a bit of hush for a buzz track.'

Again, as Saeed disappeared down the road, we stood like statues, gazing into the murky depths. Fed by an underwater spring, the Adari Pool, at that time of the morning, had little to offer. With its small derelict mosque, described in the Bahrain handbook as a beauty spot, it was a favourite place for picnics. Patently visible on the bed of the pool were hundreds of empty lager cans, coke bottles, car tyres and other rubbish. A really groovy place to film pearl divers.

'For Pete's sake,' yelled John from the depths of the palm gardens away to our right, 'will you turn off that bloody tranny!'

We strained our ears. True enough, somebody somewhere was playing a transistor radio. Sound recordists need to have good hearing and frequently interrupt proceedings while distant Boeings approach. But John Hayes can hear a butterfly fifty miles away. Just as he said, somebody, somewhere, had a radio. It wasn't us.

The noise of the radio ebbed and flowed through the rustle of the palm gardens like the sound of shingle on a distant beach. As if treading on eggs, Bob McShane screwed the camera to the tripod.

'Ready when you are Mr DeMille!' he whispered.

'Come on, for Chrissake, switch that bloody radio off!' yelled John in desperation.

We looked at each other, shrugged our shoulders, pleaded innocence and said nothing.

I looked down into the murky depths of the pool and various fresh-water fish with dracula teeth smiled back at me.

'Watch it!' whispered Bob. 'They'll have your Bolex!'

'Shut up!' John shouted again from the depths of the palm gardens. 'And switch off that bloody tranny! Please!' Once again we stood in silence.

As I looked around at the deserted pool the truth dawned on me. Khalifa, beloved Khalifa, had assured me that the pearl divers still existed. More than that, he had sworn, time and time again, that he would act on my instructions, bribing, cajoling, beseeching, imploring them to turn up – before they finally disappeared – to be filmed, to be recorded, before they died out once and for all, for ever. Khalifa, himself the son of a diver, had passed the word around, had agreed payments, had made contact with his father's old buddies, the other pearl divers. Before leaving for Paris with the Emir's entourage he had sworn that, one way or another we should film the mythical pearl divers of Bahrain.

Mythical. Exactly. That was it. A cold realisation hit me deep in my stomach and the truth dawned on me as I realised why Khalifa had, so suddenly, in the midst of our filming, disappeared. It was obvious what had happened . . .

'For the last time,' yelled John. 'Will you please switch off that flaming transistor radio!'

Khalifa had, no doubt, done his best trying to organise the few reamining pearl divers. But, in the end, he had realised the hopelessness of it all. Finally, with a fierce Arab pride, and realising that

The dance of the pearl divers

nobody would bother to turn up, despite his cajoling, threatening and bribing, he had chickened out. The truth of the matter was that the pearl divers of Bahrain either didn't exist any longer, or simply didn't want to know.

'Oh, come on! Give me a break!' shouted John. 'Do I or do I not record this buzz track? Switch off that bloody tranny!'

'It's a Dodge,' said Peter.

'Ford,' said Bob.

'Perkins Diesel,' said Peter.

We all strained our ears. Behind the tinny tinkle of the distant radio we could just hear the irregular straining of a very old diesel engine revving in bottom gear. The engine got louder and so did the music.

'Turn over!' I said.

'Sound running,' said John.

'Speed!' said Peter.

'Five ninety six, Take One,' said Julia slapping the clapper board.

And we were in business.

Sure enough, throbbing along the dusty road towards us, clanking and clanging and lurching like a life-boat on a high sea, came the oldest charabanc in the world. It was built on a timber framework and looked, it struck me, rather like an Elizabethan cottage on wheels. It swayed towards us through the palm gardens, the engine revving and roaring, never getting out of bottom gear. The music, every moment, becoming louder and louder.

We filmed the charabanc as it arrived, packed to the roof with pearl divers singing their hearts out, banging drums and clashing tiny cymbals. The single-decker charabanc did a broad arc around us. When the old engine spluttered to a standstill, the singing continued as the divers helped each other off the bus.

Some of them were blind from years of salt water and the harsh conditions of the old existence. But they sang their songs with all the gusto of a Welsh rugby football team returning home from a triumphant away win. The youngest of them could have been aged fifty; certainly no less. Most of the men were much older than that; seventy or eighty years old. Their faces were gnarled, their heads shaved, and it was difficult to tell exactly how old they might have been.

But one old blind man seemed to have a special place in the group. I noticed the gentle, attentive way the other divers helped him climb down from the bus. His old eyes had that fixed, unwavering milky stare of total blindness. His voice, as he sang along with the other men, was a hoarse, rasping, nasal fortissimo. His name, Fanshawe told me, was Allun. He is not simply the leader of the divers, but is revered, and regarded as the spiritual centre of the community – almost like a guru amongst them.

The divers descended one by one from the charabanc and the atmosphere took on the feeling of a ritual. They ignored the camera crew, hardly aware of our presence, and carried on a precise pattern, in a sequence of events they had obviously done time and time again, like a celebrant at the Mass.

The song they were singing was called 'Fugiri' – one of the old sea shanties about working on a pearling dhow. 'Fugiri,' apparently, was to do with pulling in the anchor.

But there was no anchor. So, instead, as they sang, they fixed a long rope to the wheel of the bus and pretended to haul on that instead.

The movements of the dance were slow and deliberate. The work songs had derived from aspects of life aboard a pearling dhow, and it was fascinating to see how the inflexions of the voice and movements of the body over a period of time had become codified into music and dance.

Their voices were deep and gutteral. When the rope was stretched out, the divers knelt on the sand either side of it, facing each other in two long lines. They all grasped the rope and uttered a low groan which grew and grew into an enormous crescendo. Then, with the roar of a lion, they gave a unison cry of whatever is the Arabic for 'Heave-Ho!' and yanked up their arms, making the rope snake out like a wave crashing on to a reef.

Then with a chinking of finger cymbals and an increase in tempo the dancing took on a different, livelier mood. It was structured on a 'call-and-response' pattern, like a lot of slave songs from the plantations of America and the work songs of the railroads. Old Allun, with his croaking bark, dominated the singing; all the other divers chanted the refrain.

To see all those old divers going through their songs, singing and dancing and having a rare old time, was both immensely exciting and intensely pathetic. Even on dry land they were re-living a traditional and terrifying way of life – not romantic, or exotic or photogenic – but cruel, savage and dangerous.

But the remnants of that way of life were still there and in the harsh voice of old blind Allun there was dignity, power and a fearsome energy.

We were so busy filming the dancing that we had failed to notice Saeed's return in the duck-egg blue truck. He let down the tail-board and heaved from the back of the truck a bulging sack smelling of fish.

'Me get!' leered Saeed, flashing his tin teeth, 'from Fish Market.'

Bob slashed open the sack with his Swiss Boy-Scout knife and hundreds of oysters spilled out. With total frenzy, Saeed, acting on Khalifa's instructions, started to hurl handfuls of oysters into the pool. At the same time, with much shouting and yelling, other divers were stripping off and plunging into the water to retrieve them. Sub-aqua divers encased in black rubber from head to toe arrived with an old Bolex underwater camera. True enough, Khalifa had fixed everything, just the way Walt Disney had done it.

But, although we went through the motions, the whole set-up was one big fraud and had no more veracity or relevance to life at sea than a rowing boat on the Round Pond in Kensington Gardens.

I went over to old Allun who was now having his lunch. The divers had come prepared for the day, like a work's outing, bringing pots and pans and even firewood for a picnic. They cooked up their traditional dish of rice and fish and the dancing had given them an appetite. With great difficulty, and with Ali interpreting, I explained how very grateful I was that Allun had gathered together all the old pearl divers. But what I really wanted was to film them at sea – for real – not to see them acting out an old routine on dry land.

It was not possible, he said.

It was winter in the Gulf. The sea was too cold. The divers were now old men and even the younger of them would be unwilling and, indeed, unable to stay under water in the cold this time of year.

I tried again. If we could find a dhow by the following day (the final day of our filming schedule and our last chance) would he, Allun, come out to sea with us on it and bring some of his friends?

That too was impossible. All the divers had other jobs now – those, that is, who were still young enough to work. They would be needed in the BAPCO Oil Refinery, the ALBA Aluminium works, on building sites, and a dozen other jobs. It would not be possible for them to stay away from their work. They had already turned out for us at

Pearl diver with his nose-clip

the Adari Pool. There was no possible hope that they would turn out for us again.

'But,' I said to Allun, 'the divers would turn out again for *you*. If *you*, their leader, asked them, surely they wouldn't refuse?'

Allun was a very old man. Like most of the other divers, I knew he had not been near the sea for years. But I also knew that what we had just filmed, the ritual with the rope tied to the bus and the songs and dances, meant a lot to him – to all of them. They were proud of their songs, they were proud of their seafaring past, they were proud that their fathers and forefathers for generations and generations had fished the pearls from the sea, had suffered the hardships, had worked as a community and were still held together by their songs alone. These songs were important to them and should be preserved. Allun was old. So were all the other divers; when they died their songs would die with them.

A few miles away were the hotels, the office blocks, the intercontinental airport and the satellite tracking station of modern Bahrain. Allun and his friends were all that remained of the old world, the traditional way of life stretching back for centuries, to the trading dhows of the merchants, to the invasion of the Portuguese, to the *Arabia Felix* that attracted the Romans in their quest for pearls, to the great kingdoms of Assyria and the Euphrates and ultimately to Abraham and the Flood and the legend of Gilgamesh plucking from the sea bed the 'Flower of Immortality' itself.

The new pearl, the black oil beneath the desert, was a newcomer to Bahrain – an upstart, discovered less than forty years ago. The old wealth, the pearls from the ocean bed, had been around for 5,000 years; rather longer. Before it was too late, and before that way of life vanished, would it not be a good idea to film things as they used to be?

Allun sat silent for a moment and thought about what I had said. There was a sickly irony in trying to describe film-making to a blind man, in attempting to present Television – the most ephemeral, disinterested, voracious and selfish of all media – as caring in the least about a way of life everyone was well rid of. But though his milk-white eyes knew nothing about the idiocies of television programming, Allun appreciated that I was concerned, that the film crew were concerned and that Fanshawe – regardless of whether or not he eventually composes a Symphony of Pearls and Oil – was also concerned, had made several attempts, and wished to record the songs of the pearl divers *at sea* more than anything else in the world.

On that day, round the Adari Pool, the pearl divers had come to us. 'Tomorrow,' I told Allun, 'I and the film crew will be at the old harbour in Muhurraq at dawn. We shall wait there for you and, if necessary, we shall remain there waiting for you right through the day, until the sun has set, the light has gone and it is time for us to board the plane and return to London empty handed.'

Over dinner, that final evening, the mood was hardly one of jubilation. I felt there was a sporting chance that one or two divers might turn up, but it all depended on Allun. No diver would so much as move a muscle unless Allun told him to.

Most of the film crew were non-drinkers – a situation so rare as to be unique, for I know at least one BBC crew where the sound recordist flatly refuses to travel to any location unless it has Michelin's five rosettes and six tureens, and who only covered the Bayreuth Festival so that he could subsequently talk about the *Schloss Staufenberg Spätburgunder-Weissherbst Trockenbeerenauslese '67* he'd consumed – so when John Hayes ordered an ordinary carafe of red wine that evening, it was an indication that we

Hoisting sail on a pearling dhow

were drowning our sorrows in a big way.

The Hilton, which had only opened a few weeks before our arrival and was still going through the inevitable teething troubles, was staffed very largely by diminutive Indians. The smallest of them all was one of the bell-hops who helped us load and unload our camera equipment each day. A badge bearing his name was pinned to the lapel of his smart brown uniform. It said, 'Muhammad Ali'. Being so tiny he tended to drop things rather than carry them, but maintained, throughout our stay, a passionate interest in our film and wanted to be in it.

'I see *Ten Commandments*. Very lovely colour. Make the water go like theeez,' and he would spread his arms expansively every day, dropping the box containing the zoom lens, 'and Moseeez walk across in very lovely colour. And I like *Ben Hur*, with Steeef and Boiled and Heart and Chestin. Me be in your Feeelm like Heart and Chestin!'

We said cheerio to him on our way into dinner and noted with horror that the waiter on our particular table that evening was another jittery little Indian whom we had learned to avoid. Like Muhammad Ali with the camera boxes, he too dropped things. That evening he spilled the wine all over John's arm.

'This sleeve is corked!' said John, wringing out his cuff. But by then our waiter was in tears and could not be consoled, fearing that Nicky Hilton himself would come and fire him. As he mopped up our table, shaking like a leaf and sobbing quietly, I noticed his name-tab said 'Paniker'.

It was one of those evenings.

Allun was not there at dawn, and although we hung about shivering in the grey light we seemed to be the only souls around. We waited and waited, but still there was no sign of him or indeed of anyone else, except a few fishermen sorting out their nets.

A pearling dhow sets sail

After a couple of hours I left the crew on the quayside and found a telephone in the Harbour Master's office. I called Sheikh Esa's private number, having totally forgotten that for most people it was still the middle of the night. With only the hint of a yawn, and as courteous as ever, he apologised, but said he had no idea where I might start looking for old Allun. I telephoned half a dozen other people, but still no luck. Allun, they all said, lived somewhere in Muhurraq. Where? Nobody knew.

A Coast Guard came in and handed me a cup of sweet mint tea.

'Have *you* any idea where I might start looking

David Fanshawe records the singing pearl divers at sea

A pearling dhow sets sail

for an old blind pearl diver called Allun?' I asked him.

'I'm very sorry,' he replied, 'I don't know. But why don't you ask all those other pearl divers on that dhow over there?'

I looked out of the window towards the harbour. There, about to cast off, was an old pearling dhow, jam-packed with divers. As I rushed back to the quay I could see some of the divers carrying old Allun aboard. By the time I reached the crew, the dhow was half way out to sea.

With a cry of 'Follow that dhow!' we threw our camera equipment into a Police launch and raced after it. In the night, I realised the wind had veered round to the other direction and, sensibly, the divers with their intimate understanding of tides, currents and so on, had decided to assemble the other side of the causeway and were now heading out to sea and the pearling beds.

As soon as we caught up with them we started filming and Fanshawe began taping their songs. Each action on the dhow, pulling up the sail, hauling on the anchor, fixing the oars and rowing from one pearling bed to the next had its own song or chant or shanty.

We came alongside the dhow and, taking our lives and many thousand pounds worth of camera equipment in our hands, jumped aboard. The open deck was crammed with men; the same men as we had seen the previous day at the swimming pool. But they all looked twenty years younger, for this time their singing and dancing had no make-believe about it. This time – possibly for the last time ever – they were doing it for real.

'Why did you come today?' I asked one of the divers.

'Because Allun told us to come, of course,' he replied.

As they manhandled the boom, hauled on this rope and let go on that one, I remembered what Khalifa had told me about the old days when his father had been a pearl diver. Then, he had told me, there had been dozens of pearling boats going out during the season.

But year by year, as the oil industry flourished, fewer and fewer dhows went to sea. In any case, cultured pearls from other parts of the world had wrecked the market for Bahraini pearls. Also, with the outbreak of war, and the economic problems preceding it during the 1920s and 1930s, there wasn't the money around any more to spend on jewellery.

Another reason for the decline of the pearling fleets was the simple, basic fact that pearl diving was a harsh and dangerous life. Generation after generation of divers, in a feudal relationship which was virtually slavery, had worked during the season for the captains of the pearling dhows. It was the captains, and the merchants who benefited from the life, not the pearl divers themselves. The actual divers and their families knew unbelievable hardship. At the beginning of the pearling season, in order to support his family, while he went to sea, a diver would ask the captain of the dhow for an advance of so many dinars. If, by the end of the season, the diver had failed to work off that sum, then it was carried over to the following year, and so the debt increased. If a diver was injured, or killed, or became too old to work, then his debts would be inherited by his sons. Whole families mortgaged their children and grandchildren because, if they wished to survive, they had no alternative. Additionally, the dhow captains needed provisions from merchants and, in their turn, ran up huge debts involving enormous rates of interest.

The iniquitous situation reached such a pitch that, fifty years ago, Sheikh Hamed abolished the special

PEARLING DHOW

PEARL DIVERS

PEARL DIVER

THE PEARL HARVEST

PUTTING UP THE SAIL ON A PEARLING DHOW

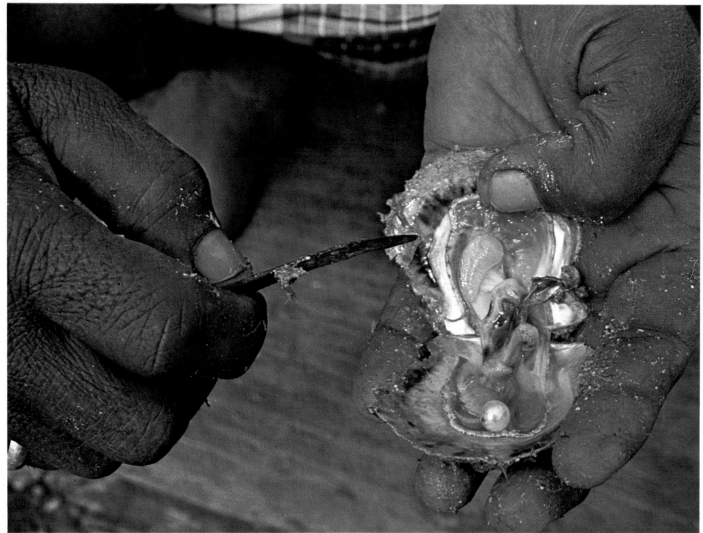

'Diving Court' which had been heavily biased in favour of the merchants and sea captains. He decreed that henceforth matters should be dealt with in the normal way by civil courts. He reformed the entire system, banned the feudal control the merchants exerted and, most important of all, ruled that the debts of a diver died with him.

But, however far-reaching the reforms, pearl diving remained a dangerous life. Beneath the waters lurked sharks, sawfish and – if you listen to fishermen who have a tendency in Bahrain to exaggerate as much as fishermen do anywhere else – monsters the size of Moby Dick. But, apart from the blue jelly-fish, which is a genuinely feared hazard at certain times of the season, the real pressures came, quite literally, from the sea itself.

By tradition and by law, divers in the Gulf are forbidden to use any form of breathing apparatus, wet suits or diving equipment. Their only help comes from a nose-clip made of bone which is clamped over the nostrils. Consequently, sharks or no sharks, there is immense pressure on the lungs, eyes and blood-vessels. Brain damage, blindness, deafness and respiratory problems are sooner or later inevitable and as we filmed we realised that many of the divers working on the dhow were living proof of this, the older men especially.

Khalifa had told me that as many as eighty or one hundred men would go to sea on each pearling dhow, living rough, sleeping on the open deck. They could be at sea for three or four months perhaps, living off only rice, dates and fish. Fresh water was not always the problem one might imagine. Dotted around the Gulf are many underwater springs and when fresh water was needed, divers could sometimes swim to the ocean bed and collect the fresh water in leather bottles before it bubbled up and mixed with the salty. The name Bahrain, I was told, means 'two seas' and,

since the dawn of history the island was a stopping off point for traders for this very reason.

At the pearling bed the dhow dropped anchor and the square-bladed oars were lashed to the sides of the boat, projecting out over the water. Each diver worked in conjunction with a *Saib* who remained on board throughout and was responsible for pulling the diver to the surface. Each *Saib*, naturally, tended to be thick-set, with powerful muscular shoulders. The divers, on the other hand, were of smaller build, thin and wiry. The degree of understanding between the *Saib* on the deck and the diver at the sea bed is not simply a working relationship like you would find, say, between the driver and conductor of a bus, but of vital importance; the diver's life depends on it.

The divers stripped off their clothes down to the bare minimum; black cotton shorts and the nose-clip pressed over the nostrils like a small wishbone. The oars stuck out horizontally over the water, tied securely. As we watched, filming the complete sequence, two ropes were slung out over each oar. At the end of one rope was tied a sort of basket, like a string bag. The other rope dangling over each oar had an iron weight or a heavy stone on the end. This was looped around one ankle and as the weighted ropes were released by the *Saib*, the divers sank quickly to the bed of the sea.

The surface of the water over the pearling bed was calm and we could just make out the skinny frames of the divers far beneath us, searching the sea bed, their limbs moving as if in slow motion, like some ghostly sea-creature, collecting the oyster shells in the basket slung around the neck.

Although the temperature of the water makes diving easier during the actual summer, the divers still managed to stay submerged in the comparative cold of February for what seemed to me like an eternity.

Khalifa, I remembered, had said that his own father – who was considered a very good diver – could stay under only for about one and a half minutes – two minutes at the most. But anyone who has tried holding his breath swimming under water knows that even a few seconds is difficult enough. Why then, I had asked Khalifa, was it forbidden by law for the divers to use aqua lungs and air cylinders, which, to me, seemed a much more sensible way of doing things?

His reply had shaken me. The obvious answer was by no means the only one. Divers are denied 'artificial' help because rich merchants, who could afford expensive equipment, would have an unfair advantage. That was one explanation.

But beyond that, although nothing was explicitly stated, you could feel another reason – that gathering pearls from the sea was something more than just a way of making money; not just an industry like getting oil from beneath the desert. Pearling signified more than that. It was a tradition, perhaps the principal reason for the ancient world of Dilmun; it was a way Khalifa's father and forefathers had lived for many centuries; it was based not on the

get-rich-quick world of Twentieth Century oil, but on a day-in day-out working relationship between the island and the water surrounding it; between the diver and the sea.

I had, at the time, accused Khalifa of being a young romantic; a modern Bahraini going dewy-eyed about his ancestors. My explanation would be that pearling was disappearing for one very sound reason: because it was barbaric, like child-labour in coal mines in England. It was gone and good riddance to it and if Khalifa went all soppy about it, he was being as unrealistic as those who buy antique oil-lamps and convert them to electricity, and nail imitation fibre-glass oak beams to the ceilings of their country cottages to make them more realistic. We all like the benefits of the Twentieth Century and tend to forget that the picturesque way of life of earlier generations which we so much envy was usually pretty gruesome at the time.

'Perhaps there's a grain of truth in that argument – like the grain of sand that goes to make the pearl inside the oyster. But,' Khalifa had said, 'we all know that pearl diving was a very hard way of life. We all know that many years ago the profits went into

138

the wrong pockets, that there was terrible injustice, serious injury very often, and that only the rich merchants got the real rewards and the divers themselves who took all the risks, working from dawn till dusk, getting very little themselves. I am not denying that.

'But I wish you could have been with me here in Bahrain when I was a child, when I would stand on the quay at Muhurraq along with the children and families of the other divers, and watch my father and all the other men setting out. When the pearling fleets went out to sea or returned, we would all stand on the quay singing the traditional songs, praying for their safety and for a good pearl harvest. We knew the ships would be away for three or four months, maybe. We knew the hardships of the life, weeks at a time, with fifty, sixty or even a hundred men living rough night and day on the open deck. We knew there would be accidents frequently and that our fathers and brothers might never return.

'But when I was a child no higher than your knee, I used to pray and implore my father to let me go to sea with the fleet. And when I was old enough he sometimes let me do that and my job was to make the coffee for the captain and to rush around the deck helping with the sails when the wind changed. And in those days, not so very long ago, as a child, I would watch all the dhows in full sail, and hear the men singing the old songs all together, and listen to the music wafting across the open, flat sea, as the fleet sailed from one pearling bed to the next. And that, I tell you, was something really good, something really beautiful; and these days it saddens me to see it all disappearing.'

Some of the old divers, with a degree of exaggeration that is forgiveable, claim that one hundred years ago, when their grandfathers went pearling, there would be as many as a thousand boats setting out each year for the oyster beds. But although fifteen hundred boats in the fleet was perhaps nearer the truth, that number had dwindled to five hundred by 1930, just before oil was discovered in Bahrain, and became the dominant economic force of that part of Arabia. More recently, by 1950, the fleet was reduced still more to only a few dozen dhows. And, looking just a few years ahead into the future, only one or two boats will remain – to take tourists for a trip around the island.

When that happens it will signify the end of a way of life that has survived completely unchanged since the legend of Gilgamesh and the beginning of recorded history, something that existed even before that unknown Assyrian scribe of 2000 BC happened to mention an invoice for a bag of pearls in his accounts and described them as 'fish eyes from Dilmun.'

Peter's harsh whisper out of the corner of his mouth, as he kept his eye to the view-finder, disrupted my sentimental musings.

'Where the hell are the divers now?' he said. 'They can't *still* be down there surely?'

As soon as the weighted rope takes them to the sea-bed, the divers hitch the basket around their necks and swim around searching for the oysters. Their only contact with the boat is the faintest tension on the rope tied to the basket. The diver collects as many oysters as he can. Then, when his bursting lungs can stand it no longer and with the stifled pulse of his blood hammering in his brain, he tugs sharply on the rope. Instantly – for a moment's delay can produce terrible physical damage to the eyes, the ear-drums and the brain – the *Saib* on deck hauls in the rope as fast as he can. Grabbing hold of the basket of oysters, the diver at the other end of the rope, is pulled up from the oyster bed before he blacks out from lack of oxygen and the

pressure of the water. Surfacing rapidly from this depth, which can sometimes be as much as twenty or twenty five metres, is equally hazardous.

There was a sudden tugging on one of the ropes and one of the 'pullers' on deck started hauling for all he was worth. Peter panned the camera and we caught the first of the divers as his shaved head burst up through the surface. Panting and gulping in the air, he hung on to the weighted rope while the *saibs* pulled up the other divers, gathered all the baskets of oysters and, with a massive unison crescendo raised them high and brought the oysters crashing on to the deck.

All day and every day the divers would do the same thing again and again, with only a few minutes' rest between dives. The divers do not eat at all while working; it is considered bad for their health. At sunset the crew eat their meal and settle down to sleep on the open deck.

Leaving the oysters until the following morning makes the shells easier to open. This is done, by tradition, in complete silence with a sharp, hook-bladed knife under the beady, watchful eye of the overseer. Sometimes it is possible to open a thousand

shells and still fail to find a pearl. At other times, if the oyster bed has not been touched for some time, there could be a tiny pearl in every three or four oysters. The pearls are collected and taken to the captain who wraps them in squares of red cloth – the best way of showing off their colour. Then the remains of the shells and the oysters are thrown overboard, in the belief that this will nourish the sea once again.

We filmed throughout the day, not only the diving and the opening of the oysters, but the songs covering every aspect of the work at sea. With so many people crammed into one boat for so many weeks at a time, it was easy to see· why the divers constituted such a tightly knit community, why they persisted, almost as one enormous family, in meeting even on dry land to sing the old songs and to swop stories the way old soldiers still talk about battles long ago.

At the end of the day, as our launch turned and headed home towards the island, we looked back across the placid water at the pearl divers – one distant solitary boat, seeming to hover half way between the sea and the sky. Fading away behind

us we could still just hear the divers singing, the only
accompaniment being the elaborate and complex
cross-rhythms of their handclapping, the thump of
a double-headed drum and the magical sparkling
clash of small brass finger-cymbals. Nothing else
was visible except the pearling dhow. In the grey
February light the sky was reflected in the calm sea
so that the horizon became a hazy and imperceptible
line, impossible to tell where the one met the other.

For a moment we switched off the diesel engines
of our launch and listened. Our motor spluttered to
silence and we strained our ears and looked back in
the direction of the music. Drifting across the water,
the rhythm of their clapping, their voices and the
shimmering of the finger cymbals came and went
like the breeze that rustles through the palm gardens.
We looked back into the grey light, but although
we could still hear the music far away, the pearl
divers were nowhere to be seen.

Acknowledgements

Throughout our work in Bahrain, preparing and
filming ARABIAN FANTASY the crew, David
Fanshawe and myself were given endless
cooperation, kindness and courtesy.
Many people, both officially and informally, went to
considerable trouble on our behalf. We owe them an
enormous debt of gratitude. But, in addition to those
mentioned in this book, I should particularly like
to thank:—
H. H. Sheikh Issa bin Sulman Al-Khalifa, Amir of the
State of Bahrain; H. E. Sheikh Hamed bin Issa
Al-Khalifa, Heir Apparent; The Minister of
Information, H. E. Tarek A. Al-Moayyed, and the
Superintendent-General, Sheikh Esa bin Mohammad
Al-Khalifa, for their personal encouragement in the
project, their hospitality and their wisdom.
Nearer home, I should like to thank Brian Thompson,
Mike Jarvis and their colleagues in Namara/Quartet
Books for seeing my typescript into print. Nearer
still – for they turned my dining room into a cutting
room to make my life easier, – my thanks to Allan
Tyrer and Pat Morris, his assistant, for editing the
film with affection, genius and understanding; and to
my wife, Julia, for her constant and indispensable help.